S0-CCE-413

EX LIBRIS

LITERARY MELBOURNE

SID SYNE

T.H.

Let your voice be
delicate.
The bees are home.
All their day's love
is sunken
safe in the comb.

LITERARY MELBOURNE

A CELEBRATION OF WRITING AND IDEAS

EDITED BY STEPHEN GRIMWADE

State Library
of Victoria

United Nations
Educational, Scientific and
Cultural Organization

CITY OF
LITERATURE

hardie grant books

PUBLISHED IN 2009
HARDIE GRANT BOOKS
85 HIGH STREET
PRAHRAN, VICTORIA 3181, AUSTRALIA
WWW.HARDIEGRANT.COM.AU

IN ASSOCIATION WITH
STATE LIBRARY OF VICTORIA
328 SWANSTON STREET
MELBOURNE, VICTORIA 3000, AUSTRALIA
WWW.SLV.VIC.GOV.AU

CATALOGUING-IN-PUBLICATION DATA IS AVAILABLE FROM THE NATIONAL
LIBRARY OF AUSTRALIA.
LITERARY MELBOURNE: A CELEBRATION OF WRITING AND IDEAS
ISBN 978 1 74066 789 0

TYPESET IN 10/15 PT HOEFFLER TEXT ROMAN

COVER DESIGN BY PETER LONG
COVER PHOTOGRAPH BY SEARS' STUDIOS, FOUR SHELVES OF LEATHER BOUND
HISTORY BOOKS, GELATIN SILVER PHOTOGRAPH, C. 1910, COURTESY OF THE
STATE LIBRARY OF VICTORIA
TEXT DESIGN AND TYPESETTING BY PETER LONG
PRINTED AND BOUND IN CHINA BY C & C OFFSET PRINTING CO. LTD

10 9 8 7 6 5 4 3 2 1

SUPPORTED BY THE VICTORIAN GOVERNMENT THROUGH ARTS VICTORIA
AND THE CITY OF LITERATURE INITIATIVE

CONTENTS

ACKNOWLEDGEMENTS

THIS BOOK IS A TRIBUTE TO THE PASSION OF A GREAT MANY people, many of them writers, scholars and publishers from both the past and present. It's a result of the collective will and the hard work that has created a culture that can stand on its own, and from the desire to reflect upon how this has come to be.

In thanking those that have brought this book to bear, I'd first like to acknowledge all those at the State Library of Victoria, from the board to the CEO and State Librarian Anne-Marie Schwertlich, to my colleagues across every field of the library's endeavour—and especially the team in the Events & Exhibitions unit, who worked so hard on the exhibition *The Independent Type*. I'd also like to honour Shelley Roberts and Margot Jones, both of whom have been essential in breathing life into this book's creation.

The kind people at Arts Victoria have been a cornerstone in the development of this book. My thanks extend from Penny Hutchinson and Greg Andrews to every arts officer who has assisted a diversity of literatures to flourish in this city, and in this state. I'd like to make espe-cial mention of the work of Stuart Koop, who has midwifed many of our recent literary developments into being. I'd also like to thank all those who were involved in organising the successful UNESCO bid—especially those on the steering committee and my co-writers who worked on the bid document: Urszula Dawkins, Greg Kratzmann and Shelly Gorr.

Most of all I'd like to acknowledge all the contributors to this book and those who have advised me along the way. This book has come into being in a very short period of time and I have relied on a number of people for assistance and advice, including: John Barnes, Joel Becker, Rosemary Cameron, David Carter, Jo Case, Michael Cathcart, Helen Chamberlin, Patricia Clark, Peter Craven, Toby Davison, Paul Eggert, Ivor Indyk, Andrea Goldsmith, Jamie Grant, Robin Grimwade, Derham Groves, Anna Hedigan, Kris Hemensley, Jenny Hocking, Deborah Jordan, Sarah L'Estrange, Pam Macintyre, Peter Mares, David McCooey, Lyn McCredden, Paul Mitchell, Elizabeth Morrison, Clive Probyn, Judith Rodriguez, Alicia Sometimes, Lurline Stewart, Lucy Sussex, Ann Vickery and Bernadette Welch. And I'd like to make special mention of Robyn Annear, John Arnold, Tony Birch, Shane Carmody, Des Cowley, Julian Meyrick, Geoffrey Milne, Agnes Nieuwenhuizen, Sue Turnbull, Chris Wallace-Crabbe, Clare Williamson, Arnold Zable and ᴕo.

This book could not have come into being without the terrific support of the team at Hardie Grant Books—my dear thanks to my editor Sharon Mullins, CEO Sandy Grant, the book's designer Peter Long and writer Dale Campisi; you've all done a wonderful job.

Finally, I'd like to thank my family and friends for their support and love, and especially Alicia and Arlo, who are my inspiration.

INTRODUCTION

FROM CREATION STORIES TO POSTCOLONIAL NOVELS, numerous forms of writing and storytelling have framed our existence, and for almost 175 years Melbourne writers—and the industry that has supported their development—have been at the forefront of establishing an Australian literary tradition. In August 2008 Melbourne was designated as only the second UNESCO City of Literature, so it seems timely to conduct a survey of our storytellers, to cast an eye over the ways they've helped us to reflect on our own lives and our shared history. To this end, this collection is a celebration of the creative individuals who have helped to forge a unique literary culture in this city. It charts the major artistic movements and historic moments, and presents some of the writers whose work has resonated in the life of both the city and the nation. And even though this book focuses mostly on work created in the last two centuries, it acknowledges the wisdom and culture that has underpinned Aboriginal experience for millennia.

Prior to European settlement Australia's Indigenous peoples had developed unique cultural traditions, many of which have been sustained over thousands of years. Various aspects of Aboriginal culture—from song cycles to paintings and rituals—underpin an understanding of country and a connection to the land. Storytelling was fundamental to the creation of their world and still plays a role in their day-to-day life.

With European settlement came a Western literary tradition. While it is not directly connected to the creation of law and the nature of survival, our literature is fundamental to the way our culture develops. Since the very first days of settlement storytellers have sought to understand and portray the world around them—this book thus follows our writers to gain an insight into our history, our culture and the way the

Australian voice came into being through the creation of its literature.

After contact had been established between Indigenous people and European settlers, a few people began to record their experiences, telling their stories in pictures and letters, and in the tales they told each other around the campfires. Important Aboriginal artists such as William Barak and Tommy McRae used their art to record and preserve culture, and to portray the world that was changing around them.

Many of the very first settlers relied on the library in John Pascoe Fawkner's hotel, while others read the newspaper that he published (which, in the absence of a printing press, was first written by hand). But for the most part settlers were reliant on the books they brought with them, or those that were sent to them from the Mother Country. As the colonies grew, so did the culture, and soon enough Melbourne and its literary scene truly began to blossom.

Victoria's history is laced with luck, and when the District of Port Phillip separated from New South Wales in 1851 gold was discovered only weeks later. From this time Victoria's fortunes were laid. The lure of riches brought hundreds of thousands of people to the state in a matter of years, and among the gold-seekers were the booksellers who created our city's literary foundation. On one particular day in 1852 three arrived on two different ships; George Robertson, EW Cole and Samuel Mullen would all play a vital role in establishing various bookshops and commercial lending libraries, and in training a generation of booksellers.

These pioneers were quick to recognise the needs of a burgeoning society, and once the framework of literary institutions had been established—the libraries built, the bookshops opened and the newspaper presses rolling—writers began to fill the gaps with colour and to reflect on the culture growing around them. Thus began Melbourne's early influence in Australian literary life.

The society that was born from the wealth of the goldrushes enabled those who settled here to reflect on their pioneering history. Writers such as Henry Kingsley, Rolf Boldrewood and Marcus Clarke captured the frontier spirit of the times, while others such as Ada Cambridge and Jesse Couvreur (also known as 'Tasma') wrote the stories of the cities. Indigenous writers are almost wholly absent from nineteenth-century Victoria, and writers from non-European cultures made only slow inroads into the mainstream. But as the intellectual life of the state matured and as more people were born in—and drawn to—this land, an Australian literary sensibility began to take shape.

Few writers approach their craft as one of nation building, but by framing the lives of their characters and by casting their ideas into the minds of readers, authors invariably chart (and sometimes alter) the progress of cultural development. By reading through the literature written across Melbourne and Victoria you can begin to see how our society has evolved.

In the early years of the colony our national identity was thought to be found in the bush, in the pioneering spirit of the early settlers; Joseph Furphy's *Such is Life* was a seminal book of this time and remains a classic to this day. The myth of the bush would remain pre-eminent for quite some time, even when other writers such as Edward Dyson returned their gaze to the cities.

For the first half of the twentieth century social realism held sway in most literary circles, moving the focus from the previous century's tales of settlers and bushrangers to those of ordinary people. Many writers associated with this literary movement were connected to and supported by Victoria's 'first family' of literature: Vance and Nettie Palmer. Victorian writers also began to consider the theme of displacement and the differences between the culture 'at home' (in Britain) and in the colonies. After the modern Australian nation was born in 1901, our literature began to reflect a greater confidence in the Australian voice and in the Australian way of being than ever before. Ironically, it would be an Australian expatriate, Henry Handel Richardson, who would become Australia's most important writer of the first half of the twentieth century.

After the goldrushes set up Melbourne's place in the nation's economic and cultural life, the next major changes in literature didn't occur until well after the Second World War, when cultural, economic and national allegiances began to shift dramatically. Because of the growth in our literary output since this time—from both writers and publishers alike—this collection is more heavily weighted to works by modern writers.

Up until the Second World War publishing was mostly controlled from the United Kingdom and most of our writers sought publication by UK firms. A healthy local publishing culture hadn't been established, and even though non-Anglo writers had made headway, it was only after successive waves of postwar migration that a greater range of cultural voices would affect the way we thought about ourselves, becoming a key contributor to the development of our national voice.

In the decades following the war would-be publishers rallied around the belief that foreign publishers had failed the needs of local literature, and these locals were intent on raising the profile of Australian writers and communicating their stories to an engaged readership. This would become one of the most important breakthroughs for both local and national literature.

A number of small, independent presses were established in Melbourne alongside the operations of large multinationals and their local agents. A unique environment was born that supported significant risk-taking in all types of publishing houses, and the growth of Australian writing was phenomenal. Cultural nationalism was reborn and this led to a great many new ventures, which included Lansdowne Press, Sun Books, Outback Press, McPhee Gribble and Penguin's Australian list.

The 1960s and 1970s were heady times for Australian cultural life and literature of all varieties blossomed across Melbourne. In this climate writers were able to experiment and find audiences like never before. In 1967 La Mama was founded by Betty Burstall and a new tradition of Australian theatre began; poetry was also beginning to find new life as it moved from the universities and into a more public sphere. Shifts in culture brought modernism into favour and the barriers between high and low culture were, for the most part, dissolved.

Since this time literary publishing—the publishing of more thoughtful fiction, poetry and plays—has experienced a variety of ups and downs, but it has remained the fare of many Melbourne publishers. But the city's literary activity isn't limited to its publishing houses; there is also a diverse range of literary practices, including theatre, poetry and the production of 'lit magazines'. Writing courses and book groups have sprung up across the state. This active grass-roots culture is serviced by a great number of independent booksellers and—combined with our multicultural society—has helped to produce a literary scene where diversity is the only real constant.

It is this history—the development of Australian literature and its distinct voices—that I have tried to capture in this collection. But the work of a mere sixty writers is extracted in this book when some 360 would actually be necessary. The nature and genesis of this collection have led to the omission of many great writers from the past, as well as numerous contemporaries. History has also, on the whole, favoured male writers, and I have not been able to rectify that imbalance. So you, the reader, are left to make your own roll call of those missing from this anthology. I hope this book will start conversations, not end them.

In addition, this collection only focuses on the work of writers, so it has been unable to showcase the broad range of individuals who have contributed to Melbourne's literary culture in other ways—early pioneers such as the founder of the State Library of Victoria, Redmond Barry; and the father of Australian bookselling, George Robertson; modern-day publishers such as Hilary McPhee, Di Gribble and Brian Johns (and the multitudes in between and after). But in addition to surveying some of the best fiction writers from the first days of settlement, we've also been able to focus on many of the literary genres that Melbourne has become famous for: poetry, theatre, crime, and writing for children and young adults.

With the help of these bold creators and independent types across many fields of literary endeavour, Melbourne has become the site of a unique literary culture, one that embraces a broad spectrum of readers and writers. I hope this book helps you explore the writers who have been central to the ways we have grown to imagine ourselves, and the ways we understand our history. I also hope that this anthology is just a starting point for further reading, and that you'll continue to seek out those writers who have shaped—and who continue to shape—the ways we think about ourselves and our relationships with each other and this city.

THE POWER OF CULTURE

STORIES, CULTURE AND KNOWLEDGE EXISTED ON THIS continent long before the modern nation was born. Aboriginal people have communicated their connection to the land and to each other through stories, art, ritual, song and dance for thousands of years.

Many Indigenous people believe that the ancestor beings created sacred sites, naming them and establishing a deep understanding of how their descendants could live in harmony with each other and the land itself. In this way traditional law was created and passed on to successive generations through cultural traditions.

Like people of all cultures, Indigenous Australians have told their stories using the technologies of the times. During the pre- and early contact periods, this was through bark and cave paintings, song-cycles, possum-skin cloaks, ritual and the oral tradition, which together signified social connections, history, creation, and both spatial and spiritual understandings of the world.

The knowledge carried in this wisdom is highly regulated, with access determined according to age, gender and background. Expressing a direct understanding of a particular part of the country, many creation stories differ for Aboriginal people across Victoria and the continent.

The functions and forms of Indigenous cultural expression don't always match European notions of writing, and very few Aboriginal people used 'literary' forms, such as the novel or poetry, prior to the twentieth century. If nineteenth-century Aboriginal people wrote in English, they were usually doing so to protest against their treatment or to petition a cause. Given the history of Australia's settlement,

and the slow pace at which the nation has embraced the richness of
Aboriginal culture, politics continues to inform the heart of much
contemporary Indigenous writing.

WILLIAM BARAK

c. 1824–c. 1903

WILLIAM BARAK WAS ORIGINALLY GIVEN THE NAME 'BERUK' and was born into the Wurundjeri clan of the Woiworrung in the 1820s. He was the son of the *ngurungaeta* (or headman) Bebejan, and as a young boy Barak witnessed John Batman's 'treaty' negotiations with his father and other elders. Barak devoted his life to representing his people as a political and cultural ambassador. He was a great artist and teacher who entertained and educated audiences through his paintings, performances and stories. He often depicted ceremony as central to Aboriginal life, and near the

middle of the scene opposite you can see a group of women beating time on their possum-skin cloaks.

TOMMY McCRAE

c. 1835–1901

TOMMY McCRAE'S DRAWINGS PROVIDE A GLIMPSE OF nineteenth-century Victoria through the experiences of an Aboriginal man. In addition to portraying ceremonies and hunting scenes, McCrae's interest in recording contemporary events was a new development in Aboriginal art, although in many ways the pictures are similar to those of ST Gill, one of McCrae's contemporaries. McCrae's earliest known drawings date from the 1860s and by the 1880s he had sold many books of his drawings, in addition to finely decorated possum-skin rugs.

Mission Station
Lake Condah
January 7. 1877

Mr Winters.
   Dear Sir.

          I want to come
back, to Wannon, I knew you
ever since I was a boy you
used to keep us live, I recollect
about thirteen or fourteen years
ago. when you used to travel
about six miles to bring us
to your place, so will you be obliged
to write to the government
to get us off this place, so if
you will write to the government
in our for us, and get us off
here, I will do work for you

(left margin)
take

not
d I

tionate friend
White

VICKI COUZENS
(KEERRAY WURRONG/GUNDITJMARA)
1960–

POSSUM-SKIN CLOAKS ARE TRADITIONAL TO THE INDIGENOUS tribes of south-eastern Australia. The designs are rich with meaning about the wearer's country and identity, and they prove these groups had a culture that was distinct from Indigenous people elsewhere. In the earliest days of colonisation Europeans traded blankets and other items with Indigenous people. From this time on the craft of making possum-skin cloaks began to wane, but it never died out. Today artists such as Vicki Couzens keep the tradition alive, making cloaks as a way of remembering and passing on traditional culture.

TUURAM GUNDIDJ

VICKI COUZENS

POSSUM-SKIN CLOAK, 162 X 320 CM (IRREGULAR), 2004

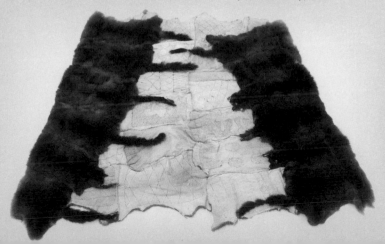

PLANTING THE SEED

L ONG BEFORE EUROPEANS DISCOVERED AUSTRALIA THEY had created myths about the Great Southern Land. For many this place was Utopia—a place where the civilised world could redeem itself; for others it was a topsy-turvy world unlike any elsewhere.

The creation of a truly 'Australian' literature would never happen while British sensibilities ruled the market. Time was needed for writers and readers to develop a relationship to their new home, and across the nineteenth century a shift began to occur.

The most successful of Victoria's earliest writers were born in Great Britain; some made Melbourne their home, while others remained in the country only for short periods. Their readership mostly considered themselves to be British—whether these readers resided 'at home' or in the colonies.

Many early novels read like travel guides, while others played up the threat and excitement of bushrangers. These pioneering stories regaled the reader with the wealth (or toil) that the Australian country promised. The characters were engaged in epic struggles against the bush and the past, and their lives unfolded within grand, complicated plots, with lashings of melodrama and romance.

These early writers did not lay claim to know what it was to be an Australian, although they were aware the culture was shifting. They wrote using what they understood from history and combined it with what they experienced firsthand. As they shed the burden of British expectations they began to see the country around them in a different light, and a new literature began to form. An 'Australian' literature began to develop slowly as writers searched for better ways to frame their existence.

GEOFFRY HAMLYN

BY HENRY KINGSLEY

HENRY KINGSLEY
1830-1876

LIKE MANY BEFORE HIM HENRY KINGSLEY TRAVELLED TO VICTORIA searching for gold, trying his luck as a miner and a police trooper before returning to England after only five years. His first novel, *The Recollections of Geoffry Hamlyn* (1859), was published within two years of his return and is a grand colonial romance that follows a community of English families as they relocate to Australia to repair their fortunes. Kingsley was one of the first to try to capture the Australian bush as it was, although his characters strongly reflected English sensibilities. Like many melodramas, *The Recollections of Geoffry Hamlyn* upholds the dream of Australia as a place for heroes to establish themselves, and like many nineteenth-century novels it provided information on the lay of the land for those brave enough to make the journey.

THE RECOLLECTIONS OF GEOFFRY HAMLYN

HENRY KINGSLEY

EDITED BY STANTON MELLICK, PATRICK MORGAN AND PAUL EGGERT,
ACADEMY EDITIONS OF AUSTRALIAN LITERATURE,
UNIVERSITY OF QUEENSLAND PRESS, ST LUCIA, 1996, PP. 191–2

A NEW HEAVEN AND A NEW EARTH! TIER BEYOND TIER, HEIGHT above height, the great wooded ranges go rolling away westward, till on the lofty sky-line they are crowned with a gleam of everlasting snow. To the eastward they sink down, breaking into isolated forests, fringed peaks, and rock-crowned eminences, till with rapidly straight-ening lines they disappear gradually into broad grey plains, beyond which the Southern Ocean is visible by the white reflection cast upon the sky.

All creation is new and strange. The trees, surpassing in size the largest English oaks, are of a species we have never seen before. The graceful shrubs, the bright-coloured flowers, ay, the very grass itself, are of species unknown in Europe; while flaming lories and brilliant par-roquets fly whistling, not unmusically, through the gloomy forest, and over head in the higher fields of air, still lit up by the last rays of the sun, countless cockatoos wheel and scream in noisy joy, as we may see the gulls do about an English headland.

To the northward a great glen, sinking suddenly from the saddle on which we stand, stretches away in a long vista, until it joins a broader valley, through which we can dimly see a full-fed river winding along in gleaming reaches, through level meadow land, interspersed with clumps of timber.

We are in Australia. Three hundred and fifty miles south of Sydney, on the great watershed which divides the Belloury from the Maryburnong, since better known as the Snowy-river of Gipps-land.

MARCUS CLARKE

1846–1881

INTRODUCTION AND EXTRACT CHOICE BY
LURLINE STEWART, WRITER AND EDITOR

MARCUS CLARKE WAS ACTIVE IN LITERARY CIRCLES IN MELBOURNE from his arrival in town in 1863 until his early death in 1881. He began working at the Public Library in 1870 and had hoped to become the Librarian, but his insolvencies in 1874 and again in 1881 prevented his application from being successful. A man of bohemian taste and mixed fortune, Clarke will be remembered for his journalism and his fiction, especially for his great convict novel *His Natural Life* (1874), in which he sought to expose both the evils of transportation and the corrupting effects of unchallenged power.

HIS NATURAL LIFE

MARCUS CLARKE

ACADEMY EDITION, UNIVERSITY OF QUEENSLAND PRESS,
ST LUCIA, 2001, PP. 144–6

IN THAT DISMAL HERMITAGE, HIS MIND, PREYING ON ITSELF, had become disordered. He saw visions and dreamt dreams. He would lie for hours motionless, staring at the sun or the sea. He held converse with imaginary beings. He enacted the scene with his mother over again. He harangued the rocks, and called upon the stones about him to witness his innocence and his sacrifice. He was visited by the phantoms of his early friends, and sometimes thought his present life a dream.

Whenever he awoke, however, he was commanded by a voice within himself to leap into the surges which washed the walls of his prison, and to dream these sad dreams no more.

In the midst of this lethargy of body and brain, the unusual occurrences along the shore of the settlement roused in him a still fiercer hatred of life. He saw in them something incomprehensible and terrible, and drew from them some conclusions of an increase of misery. Had he known that the Ladybird was preparing for sea, and that it had been already decided to fetch him from this rock and iron him with the rest for safe passage to Hobart Town, he might have paused; but he knew nothing, save that the burden of life was insupportable, and that the time had come for him to be rid of it.

From his solitary rock he had watched the boat pass him and make for the Ladybird in-channel, and he had decided—with that curious childishness into which the mind relapses on such supreme occasions—that the moment when the gathering gloom swallowed her up, should be the moment when he would plunge into the surge below him. The heavily-labouring boat grew dimmer and dimmer, as each tug of the oars took her farther from him. Presently only the figure of Mr. Troke in the stern sheets was visible; then that also disappeared, and as the nose of the timber raft rose on the swell of the next wave, Rufus Dawes flung himself into the sea.

Heavily ironed as he was he sank like a stone. He had resolved not to attempt to swim, and for the first moment kept his arms raised above his head, in order to sink the quicker. But, as the short, sharp agony of

THE
AUSTRALIAN JOURNAL
A FAMILY NEWSPAPER OF LITERATURE AND SCIENCE.

PART 257.   OCTOBER, 1886.   VOL. XXII.

For an instant the condemned man stood irresolute, as if about to speak, and then, clenching his hands, he went slowly down.

IS NATURAL LIFE.

BY
MARCUS CLARKE.

or of "Long Odds," "Pretty Dick," "Lower Bohemia," etc.

CHAPTER VIII.—(Continued.)

MAURICE FRERE and Quaid were at breakfast when the paper aining this account arrived.

ne gloom of death was on the house. Sir Richard was to be ed in a day or two, and the reading of the will would follow as as convenient.

aurice was upon thorns until he should know his fate, and d—sly, reserved, and abrupt as ever—gave him no sign. wn much into each other's company during the last two days, had grown as familiar as was possible to such opposite es, and chatted easily enough. Quaid, tired of the dreary e, and eager to get back to Thavies Inn and business, had led his work as an excuse for departure, and was to go that noon, to return for the will-reading whenever the time was for it.

Frank, sad and sick at heart, never lingered at table longer than he could help; and when the morning mail arrived, the lawyer and the soldier were alone.

Mr. Maurice Frere, coming to the tasteful concoction of the reporter for the *Globe*, first started, then swore, and then handed it to Quaid.

"Why, curse it, Quaid," he said, "I was supping at the infernal place that very night."

Quaid ran his eye down the proffered column, and started.

"I—I—I slept there," he said, a little uneasily, and clutched the paper to read.

"The devil you did! What took you there?"

"I had been to see about some law business—a trust estate at Egham," says the other, munching his toast, and talking with his eye still fixed on the paper; "and calling at the office on the way home in the afternoon, got poor Sir Richard's letter. I saw it was urgent, and so took a bed at the Bell, in order to catch the first coach."

"Did you see anything of the business, then?" asked Maurice, with that eager curiosity in matters of bloodshed which was part of his fine old English nature.

"No," returned Quaid. "I left by the half-past seven coach, and nothing was heard of it at that hour. Ah! I see the *Globe* says that the body wasn't found until nine o'clock."

"Didn't you hear *anything* then?" asked Maurice. "No now in the night? No strugglings or thumpings, you know! One

suffocation caught him, and the shock of the icy water dispelled the mental intoxication under which he was labouring, he desperately struck out, and, despite the weight of his irons, gained the surface for an instant. As he did so, all bewildered, and with the one savage instinct of self-preservation predominant over all other thoughts, he became conscious of a huge black mass surging upon him out of the darkness. An instant's buffet with the current, an ineffectual attempt to dive beneath it, a horrible sense that the weight at his feet was dragging him down—and the huge log, loosened from the raft, was upon him, crushing him beneath its rough and ragged sides. All thought of self-murder vanished with the presence of actual peril, and uttering that despairing cry which had been faintly heard by Troke, he flung up his arms to clutch the monster that was thus pushing him down to death. The log passed completely over him, thrusting him beneath the water, but his hand, scraping along the splintered side, came in contact with the loop of hide-rope that yet hung round the mass, and clutched it with the tenacity of a death grip. In another instant he got his head above water, and making good his hold, twisted himself, by a violent effort, across the log.

For a moment he saw the lights from the stern windows of the anchored vessels low in the distance, Grummet Rock disappeared on his left, then, exhausted, breathless, and bruised, he closed his eyes, and the drifting log bore him swiftly and silently away into the darkness.

ROLF BOLDREWOOD

1826-1915

INTRODUCTION AND EXTRACT CHOICE BY
PAUL EGGERT, WRITER AND ACADEMIC

ROLF BOLDREWOOD WAS THE PEN-NAME OF THOMAS ALEXANDER Browne, a failed squatter in colonial Victoria and New South Wales, then police magistrate, goldfields commissioner and part-time writer of serialised novels. Ultimately the author of sixteen novels, *Robbery Under Arms* has been an Australian classic virtually since it first appeared in book form in 1888. Through being the first writer to attempt a long narrative in the voice of an uneducated Australian bushman, Boldrewood created a tale with enduring cultural resonance. It was praised by its first readers for its excitement, romance and authentic picture of 1850s life in Australia, and Its continuing appeal and popularity has seen the tale frequently adapted for stage, radio, film and television.

ROBBERY UNDER ARMS

ROLF BOLDREWOOD

ACADEMY EDITION, UNIVERSITY OF QUEENSLAND PRESS,
ST LUCIA, 2006, P. 9

MY NAME'S DICK MARSTON, SYDNEY-SIDE NATIVE. I'M TWENTY-nine years old, six feet in my stocking-soles, and thirteen stone weight. Pretty strong and active with it, so they say. I don't want to blow—not *here*, any road—but it takes a good man to put me on my back,

BUSHRANGING AT THE BILLABONG.

or stand up to me with the gloves, or the naked mauleys. I can ride anything that ever was lapped in horsehide — swim like a musk-duck, and track like a Myall blackfellow. Most things that a man can do, I'm up to, and that's all about it. As I lift myself now, I can feel the muscle swell on my arm like a cricket ball, in spite of the——well, in spite of everything.

The morning sun comes shining through the window bars; and ever since he was up, have I been cursing the daylight, cursing myself, and them that brought me into the world. Did I curse mother? and the hour I was born into the miserable life.

Why should I curse the day? Why do I lie here, groaning; yes, crying like a child, and beating my head against the stone floor. I am not mad, though I am shut up in a cell. No. Better for me if I was. But it's all up now; there's no get away this time; and I, Dick Marston, as strong as a bullock, as active as a rock-wallaby, chock full of life and spirits and health, have been tried for bushranging—robbery under arms they called it. And though the blood runs through my veins like the water in the mountain creeks, and every bit of bone and sinew is as sound as the day I was born, I must die on the gallows this day month.

ADA CAMBRIDGE
1844-1926

INTRODUCTION AND EXTRACT CHOICE BY ELIZABETH MORRISON, HISTORIAN

ENGLISH-BORN ADA CAMBRIDGE HAD SHOWN LITERARY talent as a girl in England and, arriving in Melbourne in 1870 aged twenty-six, she soon established herself as a local author. Cambridge was at the height of her fame as an Australian novelist in the 1890s, after *A Marked Man* (1890) was published in London to wide and critical acclaim, and the book was soon after released in the US and Australia. *A Marked Man* was originally presented to the reading public as a serial in Saturday issues of the Melbourne *Age* newspaper during 1888. The story follows Richard Delavel's changing fortunes. Telling contrasts present themselves— between life in the class-ridden old world and the new 'land of opportunity', and between the immigrant and the colonial-born generations. In sum, the novel is a complex reflection on marriage ties and social obligations, and a powerful evocation of late colonial Sydney.

A MARKED MAN

ADA CAMBRIDGE

HEINEMANN, LONDON, 1894, PP. 212–13

RICHARD DELAVEL, FOR—AS HE THOUGHT—THE LAST TIME IN his life, took into his arms the woman whom nature had intended to be his mate, but whom circumstances had denied to him, and forgot everything but that he loved her and held her; and Constance Ellicott also at that overpowering crisis acknowledged herself human—a woman of flesh and blood; with the natural passions of her kind. They had neither words nor tears in this extremity; speechless, motionless, almost breathless, they stood together locked in that wild embrace—taking just seven minutes of freedom after twenty-two years of bondage and exile—one deep draught of anguish and ecstasy, such as young lovers with whom the world goes well never know or dream of. At the end of seven minutes Richard joined his daughter, and he also closed the cabin door behind him. Sue did not look at his face; she promptly obeyed the propulsion of his hand on her shoulder, and began to struggle through the crowd pressing towards the gangway.

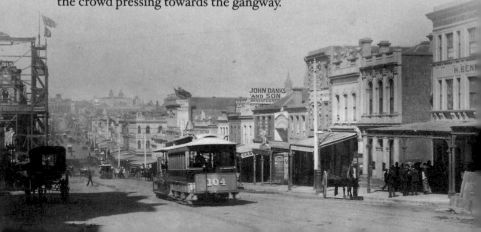

TASMA (JESSIE COUVREUR)
1848–1897

INTRODUCTION AND EXTRACT CHOICE BY
PATRICIA CLARKE, WRITER AND HISTORIAN

WHEN TASMA'S FIRST NOVEL *UNCLE PIPER OF PIPER'S HILL* was published in London at the end of 1888 it was an immediate success with critics and the public and it went into several editions. Twice-married and living in Brussels with her second husband, distinguished Belgian statesman Auguste Couvreur, Tasma was already well known on the Continent as a public lecturer on Australia. Australian readers knew her through her articles and short stories, which had been published regularly in the *Australasian* since the late 1870s, when she first adopted the pen-name, Tasma, to honour the colony where she had lived until her first marriage to Charles Fraser, a Victorian. Later she achieved another distinction when she was appointed Brussels correspondent for the *London Times*, a very unusual role for a woman. *Uncle Piper of Piper's Hill*, set in post-goldrush Melbourne among the mansions of South Yarra and in the rectory in the country town of Barnesbury (Malmsbury), portrays with humour and gentle irony the triumph of new wealth over ancestral breeding.

THE PIPERS OF PIPER'S HILL

TASMA (JESSIE COUVREUR)

AUSTRALIAN SCHOLARLY EDITIONS CENTRE,
UNSW AT ADFA, CANBERRA, 2002, PP. 114–15

THE MEETING BETWEEN MR. PIPER AND MR. CAVENDISH WAS followed by a gasp of relief on the part of Margaret and her mother. They had never dared to hope it could have been half so cordial. The truth is, that Mr. Cavendish, having bravely brow-beaten his wife the night before, having flung the whole ancestral house of Devonshire and the episcopal palace into her face, and having made her feel the height from which he was descending in allowing himself to accept her brother's— *a ci-devant* butcher's—hospitality, was by no means prepared to quarrel with a well-appointed house and its accessories. Besides, wealth was an acknowledged power, even though pork-sausages should have been its alleged first cause, and politic members of the great ruling houses in the old world had been known historically to make concessions to trade. Mr. Cavendish was prepared to make concessions too. The remainder of the loan that Uncle Piper had advanced was represented by a few sovereigns in a pocket-book stamped with the Devonshire crest. It certainly behoved Mr. Cavendish to be magnanimous, and it was with a return of the old courtly urbanity that had made him such a god in Elizabeth Piper's eyes, that he came forward in the Byronic cloak, and held out his hand to his wife's brother.

Mr. Piper's feelings respecting his brother-in-law were hardly clear, even to himself. Mingled with a half contempt for a man who could not "make his mark" in the world, was the kind of uneasy deference which, despite all his wealth and his consequence, Mr. Piper could not mentally

control in connection with the class he had been used to call "nobs."
Yet, in his position of benefactor, he was hardly prepared to "stand any
nonsense" from Elizabeth's husband, a "beggar, if you came to that, for
all his fine breeding." He bestowed, you may be sure, one of his shrewd-
est glances upon his brother-in-law, as he approached.

But there was no resisting Mr. Cavendish, when it pleased him to
adopt his *air de grand seigneur.*

"This is a real pleasure, my dear sir," he said, with ten white fingers,
the fingers of a thorough-bred hand, closing around Mr. Piper's ple-
beian knuckles. No onlooker could have supposed for an instant that
he had come with the whole of his family, in an entirely destitute condi-
tion, to live upon his wife's brother.

SEARCHING FOR
A NATIONAL IDENTITY

AUSTRALIAN WRITERS HAVE LONG SOUGHT TO LOCATE the heart of the nation and to capture it in the Australian voice. This search began to mature at the turn of the twentieth century, when cultural and political dimensions came together in the birth of the modern nation.

In 1888, the Australian colonies celebrated their first 100 years of European settlement, but the country's economy fell into depression soon after. In this milieu a particular type of national identity found a foothold in the pages of the *Bulletin*. What was aimed at readers was a masculine, matey, bush caricature that would remain ingrained in cultural consciousness for some time.

This literature was grounded in the belief that the bush was the true source of all that was noble and good in Australian life. The writers of this period honoured the land and expressed their ideas with a new-found confidence; their characters seem at home in Australia—in the country, on the coast and, eventually, in the cities.

Social realism became the dominant literary form for the next half century, and Victorians were writing, supporting and promoting a literature that supplanted melodrama with stories of everyday experience. Despite the fact that most Australians lived in cities, the focus of this new writing was slow to recognise this fact.

The federation of Australia further promoted a reassessment of the past, and some Victorian writers sought to express the displacement they felt between the cultures of Australia and England. This cultural balancing act became even more complex after the diggers' experience of the First World War, and as writers from non-English-speaking backgrounds made their way to these shores.

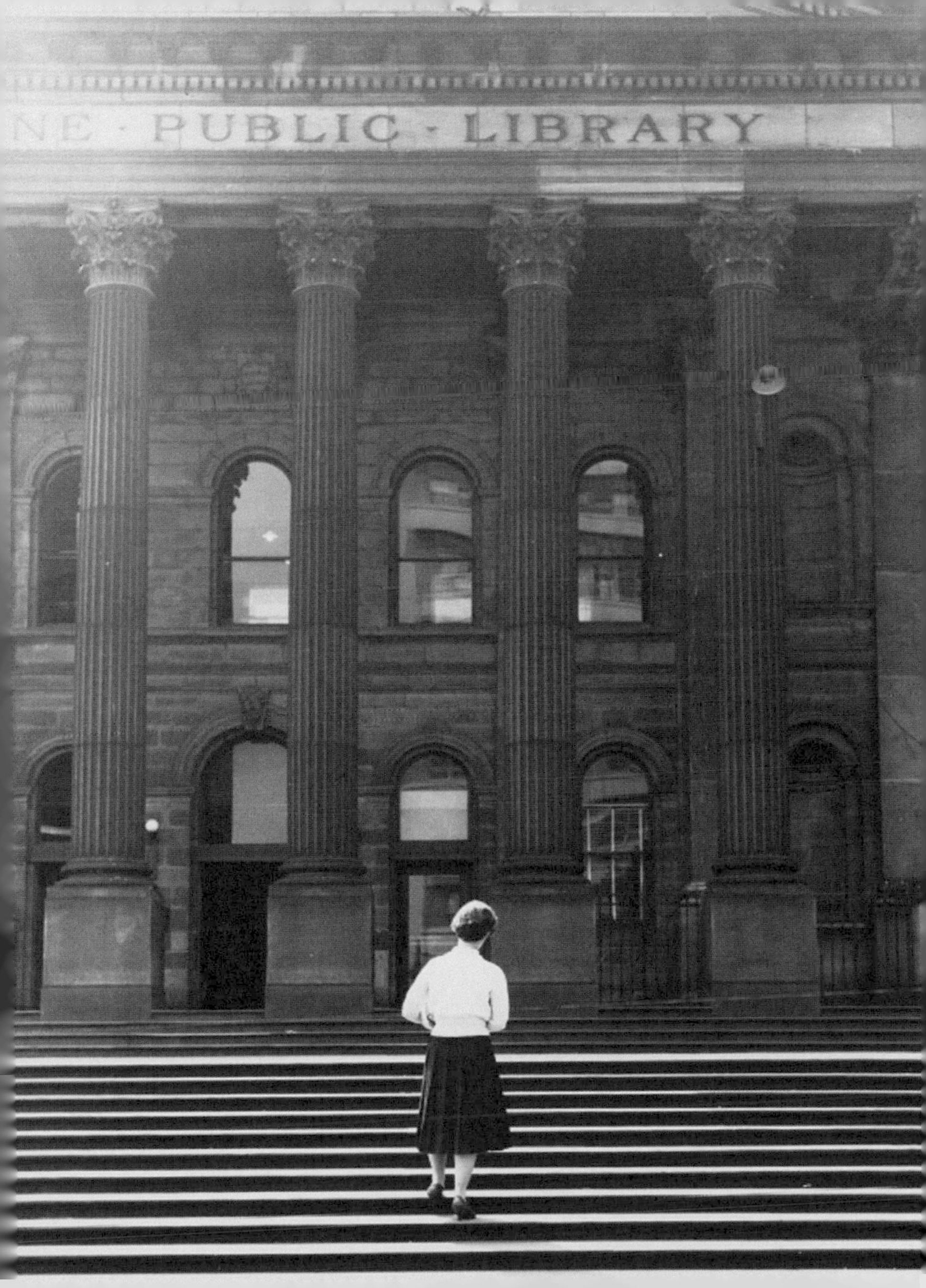
NE · PUBLIC · LIBRARY

JOSEPH FURPHY

1843–1912

JOSEPH FURPHY WAS A GOOD-NATURED, OPTIMISTIC MAN born near Yarra Glen. Furphy tried his hand at farming before buying a team of bullocks and working in the Riverina until the drought of the 1890s ended his days of plying his trade down those dusty tracks. Furphy then took work in the metal foundry of his brother (whose claim to fame is the cast-iron Furphy water tank), and it was during this time his writing began to enjoy greater success. By 1893 Joseph Furphy was contributing to the *Bulletin* and in 1897 had completed the manuscript of *Such is Life*—a tale of bullockies travelling the land, interweaved with the thoughts and morals of the narrator. This was the greatest Australian book written in this period, and was published by the *Bulletin* in the first years of the twentieth century. *Such is Life* gave a fair reflection of the people, customs and lay of the land of the Riverina. It is loaded with philosophical meanderings, and while it wasn't immediately successful upon publication in 1903, it has since been accepted as a classic Australian novel.

SUCH IS LIFE

JOSEPH FURPHY

CURREY O'NEIL, SOUTH YARRA, 1984, PP. 204-5

THOSE WHOSE KNOWLEDGE OF THE PASTORAL REGIONS IS DRAWN from a course of novels of the *Geoffrey Hamlyn* class, cannot fail to hold a most erroneous notion of the squatter. Of course, we use the term 'squatter' indifferently to denote a station-owner, a managing partner, or a salaried manager. Lacking generations of development, there is no typical squatter. Or, if you like, there are a thousand types. Hungry M'Intyre is one type; Smythe—petty, genteel, and parsimonious—is another; patriarchal Royce is another; Montgomery—kind, yet haughty and imperious—is another; Stewart is another. My diary might, just as likely as not, have compelled me to introduce, instead of these, a few of the remaining nine-hundred and ninety-five types—any type conceivable, in fact, except the slender-witted, virgin-souled, overgrown schoolboys who fill Henry Kingsley's exceedingly trashy and misleading novel with their insufferable twaddle. There was a squatter of the Sam Buckley type, but he, in the strictest sense of the word, went to beggary; and, being too plump of body and exalted of soul for barrow-work, and too comprehensively witless for anything else, he was shifted by the angels to a better world—a world where the Christian gentleman is duly recognised, and where Socialistic carpenters, vulgar fishermen, and all manner of undesirable people, do the washing-up.

HENRY HANDEL RICHARDSON

1870–1946

INTRODUCTION AND EXTRACT CHOICE BY
CLIVE PROBYN, WRITER AND ACADEMIC

HENRY HANDEL RICHARDSON WAS THE PEN-NAME OF ETHEL Florence Lindesay Richardson. Much of her fiction was made possible by the fusion of her own experience or that of members of her family with a distinctive restlessness and dissatisfaction with the given and with the present moment. This sometimes led to a keen sense of lives led in the shadow of a failed vision, of great ambition—even rebelliousness—reduced by inadequacy or personal circumstance to a dreadful state of humdrum ordinariness. This is

true of the titular hero of her epic trilogy *The Fortunes of Richard Mahony* (the three volumes were published in 1917, 1925, 1929) and also true of her first fictional creation, *Maurice Guest* (1908). This passage is from the opening proem or introduction to *The Way Home* (1925), the second volume of Richardson's trilogy. She here compares the two cultures and countries that made her world: England and what was to become the Colony of Victoria, Australia.

THE FORTUNES OF RICHARD MAHONY
PART II: THE WAY HOME
HENRY HANDEL RICHARDSON

AUSTRALIAN SCHOLARLY PUBLISHING, MELBOURNE, 2007, PP. 8–9

IF THE LANDSCAPE BEFORE THEM WAS LOVELY AS A GARDEN, it had also something of a garden's limitations. There was an air of arrangedness about it; it might have been laid out according to plan, and on pleasing, but rather finikin lines; it was all exquisite, but just a trifle over-dressed. And as he followed up the train of thought started by Mary's words, he was swept through by a sudden consciousness of England's littleness, her tiny, tight compactness, the narrow compass that allowed of so intensive a cultivation. These fair fields in miniature!— after the wide acreage of the colonial paddock. These massy hedgerows, cutting up the good pasture-land into chequerboard squares!—after the thready rail-and-post fences that offered no hindrance to the eye. These diminutive clusters of houses, huddled wall to wall—compared with the sprawling townships, set, regardless of ground-space, at the four corners of immense cross-roads. These narrow, winding lanes and highways, that crawled their mile or so from one village to the near next—after the broad, red, rectilinear Australian roads, that dashed ahead, it might be for the length of a day's journey, without encountering human habitation.

How, knowing what he knows, can he placidly live through the home day, with its small, safe monotony? How give up for ever the excitement of great risks taken and met, on grander shores, under loftier skies?

VANCE PALMER

1885-1959

EXTRACT CHOICE BY JOHN BARNES, WRITER AND ACADEMIC

VANCE PALMER—MUCH LIKE HIS WIFE NETTIE—IS REMEMBERED for his biographies of other writers and for his work on the formation of a national cultural identity. He was perhaps best known to listeners of ABC Radio at the time, for which he reviewed books from 1941 to 1956. In addition to his study *The Legend of the Nineties*, Vance also wrote novels including *The Passage* (1928), which won him the *Bulletin* Novel Competition and the Australian Literature Society Gold Medal, and *The Big Fellow*, which won the Miles Franklin Literary Award.

THE PASSAGE

VANCE PALMER

FW CHESHIRE, MELBOURNE, 1957, PP. 6–7

THE WHOLE WORLD WAS A LITTLE ABOVE ITSELF TO-DAY. ON the low, massed trees of the foreshore the afternoon sunlight lay mellow, and colours came out strongly, the yellow of sandstone cliffs, the blue smoke from hidden chimneys, the henna-red of the lighthouse dome. Apart from this surfing-beach with its suggestions of a light, holiday life, and almost hidden by a bend of the land, stood the fishing-village—half-a-dozen shanties and houses, with ricketty jetties running out into the smooth water of the Passage. Beyond rose the mountains in a wall, purple in the clear sky, yet so

near that you could almost pick out the threads of road running up their sides.

"Time to go in!" thought Lew, watching the dropping sun.

But though the fish had ceased biting he remained with the slack line between his fingers, steeped in reflection. He didn't want to go in; out there on the slowly-heaving water, where there was no craft but his own little boat, he had a sense of harmony he was unwilling to lose. An assurance flowed into him there, had always done so. Life, his own life, was good enough; he hadn't anything to grizzle over, really! That feeling of pulling against the tide, of being at war with his surroundings, was nothing but bile, after all!

He could sit there for hours, as quietly as a cowrie working in a hidden crevice on its enamelled shell, thinking of the mysteries of the reef that ran for over a thousand miles to the north, a few fathoms of water on one side of it and unplumbed depths on the other; trying to make out the orchards, small as thumbnails on the ranges fifteen miles away; letting his thoughts and sensations flow from one channel to another. The slanting sun streamed into his brown body. He was a gull skimming through the still air with spread wings; he was an anemone curled up waiting for the wash of the incoming tide; he was a carpet-shark drifting sluggishly along through the forests of waterweed.

NETTIE PALMER
(JANET GERTRUDE PALMER *NEE* HIGGINS)
1885–1964

INTRODUCTION AND EXTRACT CHOICE BY
DEBORAH JORDAN, HISTORIAN AND WRITER

NETTIE PALMER WAS A KEY FIGURE IN THE EMERGENCE OF Australian literature. Only young when the Australian colonies were federated, she shared with some of her generation an early idealism that found expression in poetry and political writings. A gifted linguist with an incisive intellect, Palmer was studying abroad during the devastation of the First World War when she and her husband Vance Palmer returned to Australia, both committed to enriching cultural debate here. Initially working as a journalist, she published a landmark volume on modern writing in Australia, in addition to one of the first Australian political biographies. She also edited the fine collection of Victorian women's writings for the state's centenary and was pivotal in the recognition of Henry Handel Richardson. She was editor, historian, essayist and environmentalist, and had a regular radio program.

of Sussex) and ot

vey accessible part

of.

new

the publication of

clear about it : who

, The Melbourne Hera

meant by sets ?

THE DANDENONGS

NETTIE PALMER

NATIONAL PRESS, MELBOURNE, 1953, PP. 45–7

WE KNOW, BOTH IN OURSELVES AND THROUGH ENDLESS repetition from outside, that we are a young country. The bones of the continent are old, but everything created by the hands of man has an unweathered look; it has not had time to merge inconspicuously into its background. Solid though it may be, it has the aspect of something unsettled and fugitive.

Yet there are places that give the illusion of an earth long tamed and humanized. Agriculture in the Dandenongs is a comparatively new experiment. There are men still living who knew the ranges when comparatively few acres of their soil had been upturned. But when our eyes rest upon the terraces of certain cultivated valleys as they glimmer between the boles of a tall forest, it is hard to believe that such a complex pattern was made in a short time. Every spreading tree—pear, apple, great walnut, Spanish chestnut, Lombardy poplar going up like smoke— has already a mellowness. Fully-grown and at home, they do not seem like strangers as they gently slope down into the red-soiled valleys.

This idyllic landscape as a whole, contrasting its planned acres with the neighbouring combe of second-growth mountain ash and ferny undergrowth, has nothing fugitive or temporary about its look. Some of the rich acres of the Patch might have been tilled for quiet centuries. It is as if their problems had all been solved, each field bearing its set fruit in due season.

Such tranquillity is, of course, an illusion. Even in a European landscape, with actual age behind it, every season brings its own problems and changes. Here in the Dandenongs the changes have been unceasing and many problems remain to be solved. Quick growth covers up mistakes of the past. You may be impressed by a towering row of pines around an old homestead, pines with a look of ancient peace about them; but you will be told that there is a more impressive and larger row further back, planted twenty years earlier, and guarding nothing but a burnt-out chimney. The first home had been built in the wrong place.

The *pinus insignis* is an immigrant, and a quick grower now that it has been acclimatised, but in quickness it is eclipsed by the mountain ash. Many hillsides cleared of this fine timber in the early days have now a second growth almost as robust as the original one, though looking more domesticated and subdued. It is this that gives a pastoral look to the ranges now, the bush itself harmonizing with the tilled country.

FRANK HARDY

1917–1994

INTRODUCTION AND EXTRACT CHOICE BY
JENNY HOCKING, ACADEMIC AND WRITER

IN 1950 FRANK HARDY'S EXPLOSIVE FIRST NOVEL POWER WITHOUT *Glory* was published by Hardy himself through his newly formed Realist Publishing and Printing company. It was the quintessential inner-city Melbourne novel—self-published, hand-sewn, thinly disguised political intrigue—and much of it written in the famous domed reading room of the State Library of Victoria. Hardy's characters bore remarkable likeness to well-known Melbourne figures, carried immediately identifiable names and created a sensation of scandal and revelation. Crude lists quickly emerged identifying characters in the book with their real-life counterparts and booksellers soon reported that *Power Without Glory* was 'selling like hotcakes'. Melburnians could not get enough of this home-grown tale of political scandal and Establishment cant. *Power Without Glory*, where to get it and who was in it, became the biggest talking point in Melbourne, even politicians were caught reading behind brown paper covers and asking each other, 'Have you read THE BOOK?'

POWER WITHOUT GLORY

FRANK HARDY

VINTAGE/RANDOM HOUSE, MILSONS POINT, 2000, PP. 17–18

ONE BLEAK AFTERNOON IN THE WINTER OF 1893 A YOUNG MAN stood in the doorway of a shop in Jackson Street, Carringbush, a suburb of the city of Melbourne, in the Colony of Victoria. The shop was single-fronted and above its narrow door was the sign CUMMIN'S TEA SHOP. In its small window stood a tea-chest with a price ticket leaning against it.

The man was of short, solid build and was neatly dressed in a dark-grey suit. His face was clean-shaven. He wore a celluloid collar and a dark tie. With his left hand he was spinning a coin. It was a shiny golden coin, a sovereign. Standing on the footpath facing him from a few feet away was a tall policeman in uniform, whose small, unintelligent eyes followed the flight of the coin as it spun up a few feet and fell into the palm of the young man's hand, only to spin rhythmically upwards again and again.

The policeman said: "This shop is on my beat. I have had complaints that you are conducting an illegal totalisator here."

A cold wind blew through the door fanning against the young man's trouser legs, revealing that he was extremely bow-legged. From a distance, the first noticeable characteristic was his bandiness, but, at close range, his eyes were the striking feature. They were unfathomable, as if cast in metal; steely grey and rather too close together; deepset yet sharp and penetrating. The pear-shaped head and the large-lobed ears, set too low and too far back, gave him an aggressive look, which was heightened by a round chin and a lick of hair combed back from his high sloping forehead like the crest of a bird. His nose was sharp and straight; under it a thin, hard line was etched for a mouth.

He was twenty-four years of age, and his name was John West.

His brother, Joe, younger by a year, stood behind him in the gloomy little shop. Joe was of similar build, but lacked the striking personality. Like the policeman, Joe was watching the coin as it spun up and down, glinting in the dull light.

After a pause, John West answered quietly in a resonant voice: "I told yer before: this is a tea shop and we only work here." His eyes were not watching the coin; they were glued on the policeman's face. "See for yerself, Constable Brogan, a chest in the window, and tins and packages of tea on the shelves and under the counter. A tea shop. Someone has informed yer wrong. All you have to do is report that somebody's made a mistake, and everything'll be all right."

"You understand, Mr. West, that we must follow up all complaints. Our informants say that nearly every afternoon, especially Saturdays, people stream in and out of this shop and don't buy any tea. I don't wish to doubt you, but – er, I have instructions to search the shop," Brogan said, and his eyes broke from the hypnotic effect of the spinning coin and met those of the young man. As they did so, John West, as though reading a message in them, suddenly flicked the sovereign at the policeman, who reached quickly and caught the coin in front of his chest. Constable Brogan looked around furtively, his cheeks reddened, and he dropped his head.

"I can see you realise you have been informed wrong," John West said. "This is a tea shop. Say that, and everything'll be all right."

Joe West had watched them tensely. He sighed when the policeman slipped the coin into his tunic pocket, saying: "I will report that, as far as I can see, this is a tea shop."

Constable Brogan spoke huskily. He hesitated, opened his mouth as if to speak again, then turned and walked down the street.

TRUTH AND THE IMAGINATION

I F VICTORIA'S LITERARY LIFE TOOK ROOT AFTER THE GOLD rushes of the 1850s, it truly blossomed after the Second World War. The war had activated significant shifts in society: Australia began to turn away from the Mother Country to Uncle Sam, a new consumer society was taking root and the atomic age had dawned.

Many Australian writers who enjoyed success late in the twentieth century were born prior to the Second World War. They knew the horrors of this time but mostly lived, studied and worked in the period of reconstruction and growth.

This postwar period heralded a range of changes across all facets of society. The numbers of students attending universities grew rapidly. As the years unfolded, opposition to government censorship saw such laws unravel. Resistance to the Vietnam War was entwined with a new libertarianism, and the second wave of feminism was gaining momentum. Victorian writers were responding to international cultural swings; many of these writers were setting the intellectual tone and were soon known around the world.

Strict delineations between fact and fiction were beginning to blur; some historians used their imagination to give history life, just as novelists were interpreting the facts to better understand our place in history. A new creative sense was brought to narrative non-fiction. Writers were using many of the same devices as their fiction-writing counterparts: they created whole worlds from source materials, inhabiting their characters in ways that stretched the historical record to create more engaging and fully realised texts.

These writers weren't interested in building up patriotic images of what Australia was thought to be, rather they scoured the historical

record and engaged with modern ideas, sometimes challenging a range
of orthodoxies. Just as in times past they were still interested in gaining
a deeper understanding of our place on this continent, but they were
less dependent on the old ways of writing history.

Since this time Australian readers have increasingly turned to non-
fiction—to our historians, critics, biographers and memoirists. Indeed,
Australian literature has seen a great rise in interest in the modern biog-
raphy and memoir—forms of writing in which Victorian writers have
been prolific. The conventional boundaries of these areas has shifted
dramatically, so that many memoirs now sit uneasily with readers inter-
ested in applying strict boundaries to both fiction and non-fiction.

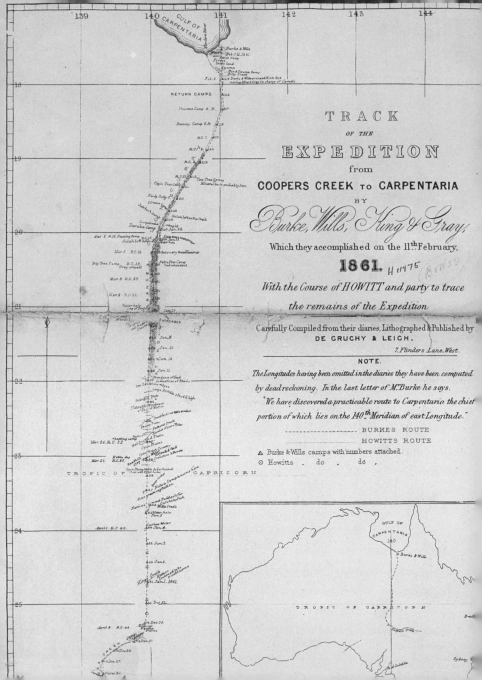

TRACK

OF THE

EXPEDITION

from

COOPERS CREEK TO CARPENTARIA

BY

Burke, Wills, King & Gray,

Which they accomplished on the 11th February,

1861.

With the Course of HOWITT and party to trace

the remains of the Expedition

Carefully Compiled from their diaries, Lithographed & Published by
DE GRUCHY & LEIGH.

7, Flinders Lane, West.

NOTE.

The Longitudes having been omitted in the diaries they have been computed
by dead reckoning. In the last letter of Mr Burke he says.

"We have discovered a practicable route to Carpentaria the chief
portion of which lies on the 140th Meridian of east Longitude."

------------------------- BURKES ROUTE

—————————— HOWITTS ROUTE

△ Burke & Wills camps with numbers attached.

○ Howitts do do.

ALAN MOOREHEAD
1910–1983

ALAN MOOREHEAD BEGAN HIS WRITING LIFE AS A JOURNALIST, becoming one of Australia's most respected war correspondents during the Second World War. He wrote a series of works on various military campaigns—these coming together as *African Trilogy* (1946)—but gave up journalism after this period. From this time on he lived in Porto Ercole in Tuscany, Italy, and wrote a number of books including two biographies—of General Montgomery (1958) and Winston Churchill (1960)—and historical narratives including *Gallipoli* (1956) and *Cooper's Creek* (1963), which won the Royal Society of Literature Prize in 1963. He was awarded the OBE in 1946 and the CBE in 1968.

COOPER'S CREEK
THE REAL STORY OF BURKE AND WILLS
ALAN MOOREHEAD
SUN BOOKS/MACMILLAN, SOUTH MELBOURNE, 1985, P. 102

FOR THE NEXT SIX DAYS THERE ARE MERELY JOTTINGS IN WILLS' diary; obviously the strain of the march left him with no energy to write. Perhaps had rain fallen they might have got through, but as things were they went on and on and there was nothing before them on the empty horizon, not a tree, not a sign of water. When they had marched about forty-five miles south-west from the creek—five miles beyond the point which they had estimated to be their absolute

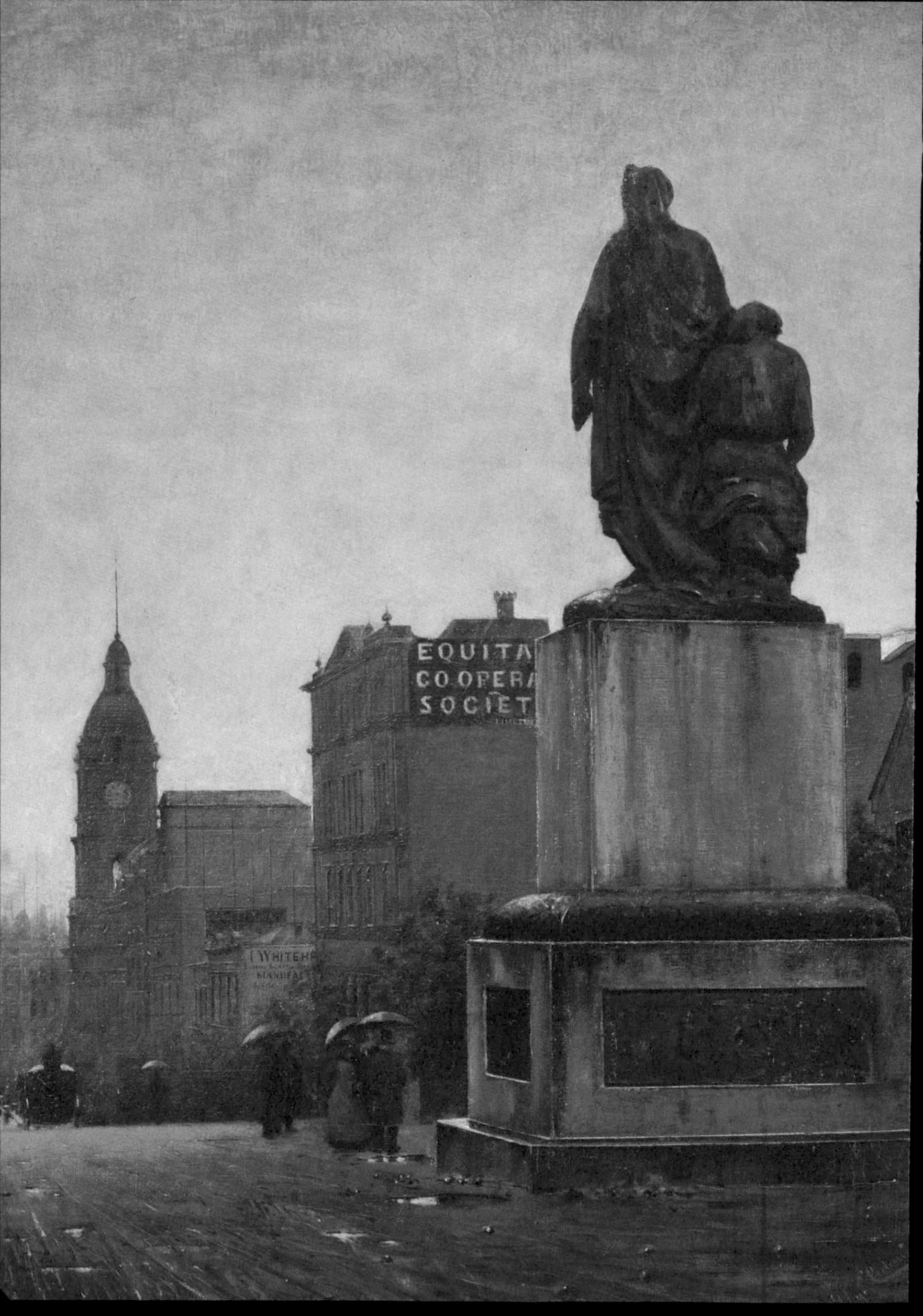
EQUITA
CO.OPERA
SOCIET

limit—they sat down among the sandhills to rest for an hour and then turned back.

Even across a gap of a hundred years it is difficult not to feel indignant. This was too hard; surely they might have been allowed, if not success, at least a little respite: a shower of rain, a pigeon such as Sturt had seen making for a waterhole, just one faint whisper of hope instead of this endless implacable rejection. The narrow margin by which they had missed Brahe at the depot had been, in the main, bad luck, and Brahe's failure on his return visit to realize that they had been there, though maddening, was a comprehensive twist of fate. But this remorseless hostility of the land itself was unfair, perversely and unnaturally so.

MANNING CLARK
1915–1991

INTRODUCTION AND EXTRACT CHOICE BY MICHAEL CATHCART, HISTORIAN, WRITER AND BROADCASTER

PROFESSOR MANNING CLARK'S epic achievement was his six-volume work *A History of Australia*. The first volume, published in 1962, declared Clark's high purpose in its defiant opening sentence: 'Civilisation did not begin in Australia until the last quarter of the eighteenth century.' Clark announced his intention to treat Australian history as a titanic struggle between three rival ideas of morality—Catholicism, Protestantism and what he rather sweepingly called the Enlightenment. But in the succeeding volumes, other great forces began to shape his cosmos. Sometimes, he wrote as if communist revolution was about to sweep across the country as a terrifying and purifying force. Other times, he sought solace and hope in the high arts or in Christianity. Clark's *History* is really one man's quest for meaning—a quest waged on the land-scape of his own country's history.

A HISTORY OF AUSTRALIA

VOLUME IV: THE EARTH ABIDETH FOR EVER 1851–1888

MANNING CLARK

MELBOURNE UNIVERSITY PRESS, CARLTON, 1978, PP. 77–8

ON FRIDAY AND SATURDAY, 1 AND 2 DECEMBER, THE DIGGERS feverishly constructed a stockade out of slabs of wood which had pre-viously done service as pit-props in their holes, and armed themselves with rifles. Those without rifles sharpened pikes. As they laboured in those balmy summer days they strengthened each other with assur-ances that a great political change was about to occur. A government corrupt to the core was about to fall. The people would no longer slave all day to 'fatten a migratory flock of mere adventurers' such as Rede and Pasley and Thomas and their offsiders. The time had come to be governed by the people's politicians and not by that mountebank politi-cian who presided over the government of Victoria. Some were heard to raise the cry of 'Victoria for the Victorians'.

Over in the camp, officers and men were showing by all sorts of ges-tures and attitudes and intemperate words their eagerness to give the diggers a taste of 'steel and lead'. Captain Pasley was more convinced than ever, as he had put it first on the night of 30 November, that 'very strong measures are necessary in this gold field, and that sedition must

be put down by force'. Conciliatory measures would only do harm; the disaffected must be coerced. On the night of 2 December he repeated again to his fellow-officers the slogan he had used earlier that week: to risk the camp was to risk the colony. At a council of war that night he and his fellow-officers decided to destroy the stockade and sweep the whole gold-field with shot on the following day.

By then the windlasses were silent; manual labour, buying and selling and even tippling had stopped. Everyone was excited and confused. On one side of the field the scarlet-shirted and white-capped men of the cavalry, the infantry and the police stood at the ready. Across the valley on the other side the 'bone and sinew' of the colony, armed with the Irish pike of yesteryear, the latest American revolver, the 'Djerid' of the Arab and the cutlass of 'Jack tar', the ploughshare and the reaping hook were also at the ready. By Saturday night the numbers had fallen from 2000 to 150 as men, for motives as diverse as the motives that brought them to that fever pitch of the night of 30 November when they swore allegiance on bended knee to the Southern Cross, drifted back to their tents. Some of the 150 who remained spent the night carousing till they lost consciousness. They slept there under the canopy of that very vast sky, not knowing that this time men with hangovers and alcoholic remorse were to be changed by smoke and shot into folk heroes.

As first light spread over the valley, Captain Thomas was telling his troops the time had come to save the colony by destroying the stockade. To achieve that the troops and the mounted police would proceed at once to the place where the revolutionary flag was flying. When the troops were within 150 yards of the stockade, they were received by a rather sharp and well-directed fire from the rebels. Captain Thomas then ordered the bugler to sound the 'commence firing!' Captain Wise, the cheerful man whom everyone loved, fell, shot in the knee, gaily telling his comrades his dancing was now spoiled forever. As he spurred on his men he was shot again and was carried from the field just as the troops climbed over the slabs into the stockade. John King, a native of Mayo in Ireland, climbed the flagstaff, pulled down the rebel flag and tore it to shreds, to the cheers of his fellow-soldiers. In the madness of the moment the soldiers threatened to murder every one of the 150 rebel bastards inside the stockade. Captain Pasley shouted above the uproar that any soldier who murdered a prisoner would be shot on the spot. Captain Thomas then ordered the firing to cease, the bugle sounded the retreat, and the whole force, together with their large contingent of prisoners, retired to the camp. It was all over in fifteen minutes.

GEOFFREY BLAINEY

1930–

GEOFFREY BLAINEY IS ONE OF AUSTRALIA'S PRE-EMINENT historians. He began his writing as an economic historian, and is renowned for the book he published with the new independent publisher Sun Books. Blainey's *The Tyranny of Distance* was published in 1966 and sought to understand Australia's history through the way in which Australia's geographical place in the world—both its distance from Europe and its proximity to Asia—affected both the Australian economy and culture. Blainey's phrase 'the tyranny of distance' has now entered the common

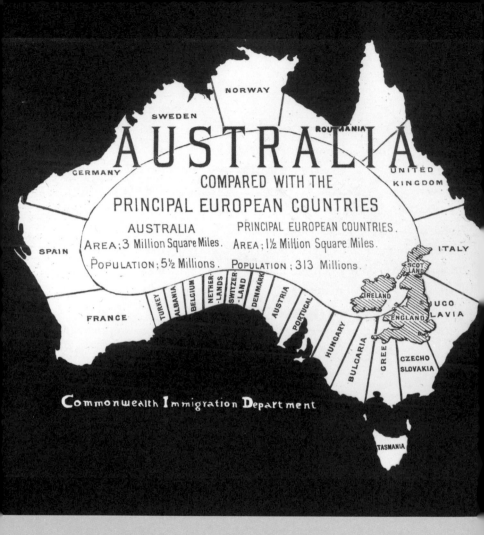

AUSTRALIA
COMPARED WITH THE
PRINCIPAL EUROPEAN COUNTRIES

AUSTRALIA
AREA; 3 Million Square Miles.
POPULATION; 5½ Millions.

PRINCIPAL EUROPEAN COUNTRIES.
AREA; 1½ Million Square Miles.
POPULATION; 313 Millions.

Commonwealth Immigration Department

SWEDEN
NORWAY
ROUMANIA
GERMANY
UNITED KINGDOM
SPAIN
ITALY
SCOTLAND
IRELAND
JUGO SLAVIA
ENGLAND
FRANCE
TURKEY
ALBANIA
BELGIUM
NETHER-LANDS
SWITZER-LAND
DENMARK
AUSTRIA
PORTUGAL
HUNGARY
BULGARIA
GREECE
CZECHO SLOVAKIA
TASMANIA

lexicon, expressing how remoteness can affect the outcome of a
situation. Blainey's other books include *Triumph of the Nomads*
(1975), *A Shorter History of Australia* (1994), *A Short History of
the World* (2000) and *A Short History of the Twentieth Century*
(2005). Blainey was awarded the Order of Australia in 1975.

THE TYRANNY OF DISTANCE
HOW DISTANCE SHAPED AUSTRALIA'S HISTORY
GEOFFREY BLAINEY
SUN BOOKS/MACMILLAN, SOUTH MELBOURNE, 1983, P. 98

MUCH OF AUSTRALIA'S EARLY HISTORY WAS INFLUENCED BY its proximity to trade routes and to promising spheres of trade. Much of its later history was influenced by the fact that it was on a limb, far from the trunk routes of world trade. By the 1830s that change was visible. Australia was becoming more a terminus and goal for shipping and less a port of call. Its shipping links with Europe were now much more important than its shipping links with Asia and the Pacific. Australia was becoming useful, not so much as a dead-end house for English criminals and a half-way house for English ships, than as a source of Britain's raw materials—wool from the land and whale oil from the sea.

GERMAINE GREER
1939–

EXTRACT CHOICE BY ALICIA SOMETIMES,
POET AND BROADCASTER

GERMAINE GREER IS ONE OF AUSTRALIA'S MOST RENOWNED critics, living in England but writing and commenting on issues of significance to Australian lives, and often challenging the accepted viewpoint. Greer was a regular contributor to *Oz* magazine from 1968 to 1971, but her major breakthrough was the publication of *The Female Eunuch* in 1970, a book espousing women's sexual liberation, and one which would set Greer up as an international 'intellectual celebrity'. Greer now regularly comments on all aspects of culture, and has written widely, with essays on Australian nationhood and Aboriginal rage, as well as books on Shakespeare's wife and the beauty of boys.

THE FEMALE EUNUCH

GERMAINE GREER

HARPER PERENNIAL, HARPERCOLLINS PUBLISHERS, LONDON, 2006, P. 70

So what is the beef? Maybe I couldn't make it. Maybe I don't have a pretty smile, good teeth, nice tits, long legs, a cheeky arse, a sexy voice. Maybe I don't know how to handle men and increase my market value, so that the rewards due to the feminine will accrue to me. Then again, maybe I'm sick of the masquerade. I'm sick of pretending eternal youth. I'm sick of belying my own intelligence, my own will, my own sex. I'm sick of peering at the world through false eyelashes, so everything I see is mixed with a shadow of bought hairs; I'm sick of weighting my head with a dead mane, unable to move my neck freely, terrified of rain, of wind, of dancing too vigorously in case I sweat into my lacquered curls. I'm sick of the Powder Room. I'm sick of pretending that some fatuous male's self-important pronouncements are the objects of my undivided attention, I'm sick of going to films and plays when someone else wants to, and sick of having no opinions of my own about either. I'm sick of being a transvestite. I refuse to be a female impersonator. I am a woman, not a castrate.

BRENDA NIALL

1930–

**INTRODUCTION AND EXTRACT CHOICE BY
ANNA HEDIGAN, WRITER AND REVIEWER**

BRENDA NIALL'S EXPANSIVE VISION OF THE EXTRAORDINARY
Boyds and their 'painting gene' pays attention to its early mem-
bers, whose graft and luck at Melbourne's founding set the
bedrock of a fortune that was safeguarded by two generations of
careful matriarchs. The money allowed Penleigh and Merric, the

parents of the most famous generation of Boyds (siblings Arthur, David, Mary, Lucy and Guy, as well as their cousin Robin) to grow up in an atmosphere that treasured labours that sat outside the normative grind of working life: making homes, gardens, intelligent conversation and, above all, art.

THE BOYDS

BRENDA NIALL

MELBOURNE UNIVERSITY PRESS, CARLTON, 2007, PP. 167–8

IN 1913 MERRIC MOVED FROM THE FARM AT YARRA GLEN, where his first experiments in pottery were made, to Murrumbeena, which was then a suburb in the making, with only a few houses scattered about in large tracts of farmland awaiting development. On a double block at 8 Wahroonga Crescent, bought for him by his parents, a house was built to Merric's design. The land had once been an orchard, and its old trees remained. Since Merric would never think of pruning a tree, they blossomed casually year after year. His house, which he called Open Country Cottage, was decidedly utilitarian, with none of the romantic spirit of Penleigh's The Robins at Warrandyte. Over the years it took on a style and character of its own. Its centre was 'The Brown Room' a large, all-purpose room, where the family had their meals, sat and talked, read and sketched. Two small bedrooms, an unlined kitchen with a wood stove, a pantry, vestibule, bathroom, laundry and verandah completed this very basic dwelling. Merric's original sketch included a drawing-room, but this was never built, nor was there ever any kind of formal garden. Trees and shrubs and unmown grass made Open Country more like a bush cottage than a suburban house. A path from the house led to a studio and workshop where Merric's inventiveness showed itself in the machines he used in clay preparation. Because the Murrumbeena and Oakleigh districts had good deposits of clay, Merric had only to dig a pit in his own garden to get the makings of his work, in his early years at least. He was self-reliant and ingenious in setting up his pottery. The 'multi-purpose clay preparation machine called a "blunger" which he attached to the big pear tree in the back-yard' was one of his inventions. Merric made his own glazes, recording successes and failures in his 'recipe book' and kept the ingredients in his studio 'poison cupboard'.

INGA CLENDINNEN

1934–

INTRODUCTION AND EXTRACT CHOICE BY PETER CRAVEN,
LITERARY CRITIC, JOURNALIST AND EDITOR

INGA CLENDINNEN IS A HISTORIAN WHO HAS TURNED HERSELF into a writer, not necessarily by writing fiction (though she tries her hand at it in parts of her powerful memoir *Tiger's Eye*), but by ensuring that the kind of non-fiction she writes—whether it's the history of *Dancing With Strangers* (2003), which is preoccupied with the encounters of the Aboriginal peoples and settlers, or her intensely probing book-length essay *Reading the Holocaust*—is always alive, in theory and in practice, to the role of the imagination. As a historian (the great historian of the Spanish dealings with the Aztecs and Mayans), she was always an analyser of

the past who was intent on incorporating the subject position—
that is, to present her subjectivity as a figure in the landscape
of potential historical understanding. Clendinnen has made this
intellectual habit of mind into more than a discipline—she has
made it into an aesthetic. In her best work we get the most power-
ful possible dramatisation of what it might mean to suffer serious
illness, to understand how ordinary Germans became entangled
in the spectre of Nazism, or to see the Australian world through
the eyes of the early white settler and the Aboriginal, by under-
standing both the difference and the shared imaginative space
of human individuality. Clendinnen is the most striking example
in contemporary Australian literature of an academic who has
become a towering intellectual figure by having the courage to
present the world of history and of contemporary preoccupation
in a way that is compatible with the challenge of the imagination.
She is, among other things, an elegant stylist and a woman of
great sensibility, though the quintessential quality of her work
is the fearlessness with which she confronts the reality of human
pain and manages to make the representation of that drama both
exhilarating and full of moral gravity.

DANCING WITH STRANGERS

INGA CLENDINNEN

TEXT PUBLISHING, MELBOURNE, 2005, PP. 6–7

ON A DECEMBER EVENING IN 1832 THE *BEAGLE* ENTERED A BAY in Tierra del Fuego and gave young Charles Darwin his first view of the famously savage Fuegians. Through the gloom he could distinguish some remarkably tall men, naked except for long skin cloaks slung from their shoulders, perched on the edge of a wild promontory, shouting and waving their cloaks. He watched as they followed the ship along the coast to its overnight anchorage.

Darwin was an eager member of the party which went ashore the next morning to meet the wild men. There were four of them, and Darwin was fascinated: 'I could not have believed how wide was the difference between savage and civilised man; it is greater than between a wild and domesticated animal ... their very attitudes were abject, and the expression of their countenances distrustful, surprised, and startled.' That vast gulf shrank slightly over the next minutes. The wild men accepted the Englishmen's gifts of scarlet cloth, which they tied around their necks, and in return they gave their own welcome. An old man paired himself with Darwin, clucked like a chicken, patted the Englishman on the breast, gave him three hearty, simultaneous slaps on the back and chest, and then bared his bosom for Darwin to return the compliment.

What to do next? Clearly words were useless: Darwin thought the men's language was no language at all, being as savage as they were, a 'barely articulate' matter of raspings and hawkings with a few gutturals mixed in. So parallel gabbling gave way to a more elastic mode of expression: competitive face-pulling. The British began it ('Some of our party began to squint and look awry'); the savages eagerly reciprocated, winning the contest when one young Fuegian with black-painted face and a white band across the eyes 'succeeded in making far more hideous grimaces'. Then they mouthed words at each other, and again the Fuegians won: 'They could repeat with perfect correctness each word in any sentence we addressed them, and they remembered such words for some time'; and Darwin paused to wonder why the savages should have a natural bent for mimicry.

Then the British reclaimed the initiative. They began to sing and to dance, and this time they struck gold: 'When a song was struck up by our party I thought the Fuegians would have fallen down with astonishment. With equal surprise they viewed our dancing.' But they recovered quickly, and 'one of the young men, when asked, had no objections to a little waltzing'. Later in the day there was more dancing, and by the evening, Darwin tell us, 'we parted very good friends; which I think was fortunate, for the dancing and "sky-larking" had occasionally bordered on a trial of strength'. The wild men had truly descended from their 'wild promontory' to mingle and dance on the beach. We leave Darwin and his company peacefully waltzing with savages in the Land of Fire.

MODERN FICTION

I N THE YEARS BOTH BEFORE AND AFTER THE SECOND
World War the political inclinations of the social realists remained
the dominant force in Australian fiction. Our writers had, on the
whole, been slow to acknowledge shades of storytelling outside
what Patrick White described as the 'dreary, dun-coloured offspring of
journalistic realism'. Yet by the 1960s the power of the social realists no
longer held sway and writers, outside of these constraints, were able to
create more modern ways of reading their environment.

In the 1960s and early 1970s culture was changing rapidly, the arts
enjoyed greater freedoms, and society had been buoyed by a growing
economy. Up until this time the 'project' of Australian literature had
begun to be more fully realised, but postwar writers sought to challenge
and broaden the understanding of what it was like to live in this coun-
try. Perhaps this could be seen as a reaction against the success of those
who had previously championed an independent nationalism.

Diversity became a key feature of late twentieth-century literature,
and experimentation became far more popular in the writing of this
period. In a world in which distances were shrinking and cultures were
mixing, modernist techniques found a more prominent place in literary
culture. New forms of storytelling were embraced and voices of author-
ity gave way to different points of view.

Writers re-imagined what it was to be Australian by using a variety
of styles, by re-interpreting history, and by situating their stories in
a range of contemporary settings. Over this period the city began to
sprawl into the province of the country, and the suburbs—both inner
and outer—became fair game for the novelists who were, on the whole,
brought up in these areas.

'Truth', in both fiction and history, became contentious territory as writers sought to represent both themselves and the inner lives of characters. The artistic culture was maturing and our writers and artists could be more provocative. Literature wasn't seen to be the place for a simplified 'nation building', especially in an era when the nation state was becoming a blurred concept. Novelists were less self-conscious about their nationality and, as the literatures of the world's cultures mixed with our own, Australian authors began to be read more widely across the globe.

JOAN LINDSAY
1896–1984

INTRODUCTION AND EXTRACT CHOICE BY
ROSEMARY CAMERON, FESTIVAL DIRECTOR

JOAN LINDSAY WAS BORN IN MELBOURNE AND STUDIED AT
the National Gallery School of Art. She married Sir Daryl Lindsay,
also a painter and the youngest son of the famous Lindsay family
of artists and writers. Joan Lindsay's mystical *Picnic at Hanging
Rock* (1967) has intrigued and confused its public for over forty
years, and Lindsay herself artfully encouraged the belief that the
novel was based on a true story. The only reality in this mystery is
Hanging Rock itself—a monolith near Mount Macedon. Everything
else is invented. *Picnic at Hanging Rock* follows the repercussions
of the mysterious disappearance of a teacher and three school-
girls while climbing the rock on St Valentine's Day 1900.

PICNIC AT HANGING ROCK
JOAN LINDSAY

VIKING/PENGUIN BOOKS, RINGWOOD, 1987, P. 33

THE FOUR GIRLS WERE ALREADY OUT OF SIGHT when MIKE CAME
out of the first belt of trees. He looked up at the vertical face of the
Rock and wondered how far they'd go before turning back. The Hanging
Rock, according to Albert, was a tough proposition even for experi-
enced climbers. If Albert was right and they were only schoolgirls about
the same age as his sisters in England, how was it they were allowed to

set out alone, at the end of a summer afternoon? He reminded himself that he was in Australia now: Australia, where anything might happen. In England everything had been done before: quite often by one's own ancestors, over and over again. He sat down on a fallen log, heard Albert calling him through the trees, and knew that this was the country where he, Michael Fitzhubert, was going to live.

GERALD·MURNANE
1939–

EXTRACT CHOICE BY IVOR INDYK, ACADEMIC, EDITOR AND PUBLISHER

GERALD MURNANE'S FIRST BOOK WAS *TAMARISK ROW*, PUBLISHED in 1974 by Heinemann and edited by Hilary McPhee. In 2008 a new edition of *Tamarisk Row* was reissued by Giramondo Publishing, restoring Murnane's original ending and bringing the book back 'into print'. Since his childhood Murnane has been a horse-racing enthusiast and a youthful imagining of racing culture provides the central point around which *Tamarisk Row* revolves. Indeed, as a youth Murnane would draw racing colours and one of his illustrations graces the cover of the new edition. In 2008 Murnane was given the Australia Council's Writers' Emeritus Award, and in 1999 he won the Patrick White Award.

TAMARISK ROW

GERALD MURNANE

GIRAMONDO PUBLISHING CO., ARTARMON, 2008, PP. 121–4

IN THE HOTTEST HOUR OF THE AFTERNOON THE FIRST STARTER in the Gold Cup appears on the track and the thousands of people standing with their backs to the city look down at their racebooks to check the colours and numbers of the field. As the voice of the course broadcaster announces each name the connections and supporters of that horse look up from the page to see the silk jacket of the rider, conspicuously alone against the waste of grass that fills the inside of the course. The sound of each name and the stately passage of each precisely coloured jacket past the stand remind the crowd that this day they have waited so long to enjoy is no ordinary holiday but a solemn occasion because despite all the ambitious claims of the resonant names and arresting colours only one horse will be famous for years afterwards while the followers of those that come within a few yards of winning will talk among themselves during those years of some trifling accident – a horse shifting ground for a few yards approaching the turn or a horse changing stride in the straight or a rider losing his balance near the post – that condemned them to remember only a victory that was almost theirs. Number one *Monastery Garden,* purple shade, solitudes of green, white sunlight, for the garden that Clement Killeaton suspects is just beyond the tall brick wall of his schoolyard – the garden where priests pray and meditate beneath the leaves on even the hottest afternoons. Number two *Infant of Prague,* alluring satin and embraceable cloth-of-gold, for the picture of the child Jesus that Clement tries to fix in his mind after holy communion. Number three *Mysteries of the Rosary,* incandescent depths of blue enclosing elusive jewelled points

or stars, for the beads that Clement rolls delicately between his finger-
tips while he meditates on the joys and sorrows and glories of Our Lady.
Number four *Silver Rowan,* a film of translucent rainy colour across the
pure green of a country much older than Australia, for the horse that
Augustine Killeaton still dreams of owning. Number five *Lost Streamlet,* a
stripe of golden brown persisting through the grey-green of remote thick-
ets, for the creek that might lead Clement to the secrets of Bassett if only
he could follow it through a confusing maze of side-streets where he sees
only glimpses of it. Number six *Hare in the Hills,* the colour of lawns spot-
ted with flowers in valleys where the birds and animals are almost tame,
for the land of Little Jacky Hare – the land that no Australian boy has ever
entered. Number seven *Passage of North Winds,* an orange-red colour that
is best looked at from a certain angle and is continually threatened by a
turbulent yellow whose true extent may be far greater than the colour it
opposes, for the miles of plains to the north of Bassett which Augustine
Killeaton once crossed and which Clement believes stretch unbroken to
the heart of Australia. Number eight *Transylvanian,* grey or the colour of
pale skin with seams or veins the colour of a precious stone from a far
country, for the endless journey of the gypsies from Egypt through the
gloomy valleys of Europe to the grassy back-roads of northern Victoria
and still further to places only they could discover because Australians
all thought their country had been thoroughly explored. Number nine
Captured Riflebird, a colour that wavers between green and purple enclosed
with gold or bronze margins, for all the rare and gorgeous birds of Australia
that Clement Killeaton only knows from books and may never observe
except in some enormous aviary copied from the Australian landscape.
Number ten *Hills of Idaho,* gold or buff the colour of endless distances

edged with the faintest stripe or suggestion of mauve or pale-blue, for the most longed-for vista of America – the shimmering foothills that all hillbilly singers and film stars are trying to reach. Number eleven *Veils of Foliage,* a striking pattern of black and silver and gold overlaid with deep green, for the glimpses of sumptuous lounge-rooms behind flashing windows overhung with shrubbery that are all Clement has seen of the homes of the wealthy people of Melbourne who work as professional punters or illustrators of magazines or projectionists in picture theatres. Number twelve *Springtime in the Rockies,* all turquoise or peacock-blue or amethyst, for the sky over the mountains on the morning of the day when a man nears the end of his long journey back to the woman he has loved since he first peeped into her backyard as a schoolboy, and wonders whether she will have pity on him after all the miles he has travelled. Number thirteen *Den of Foxes,* a preponderance of black or dark-brown with only a hint of a smouldering colour like the flash of some rare treasure or the eye of a wild dingo in an inaccessible cave, for all the secrets that Therese Riordan and the girls of Bassett will never reveal. Number fourteen *Proud Stallion,* flamboyant scarlet perversely opposed by a luxurious violet colour, for the furtive excitement that Clement enjoyed when he persuaded Kelvin Barrett to behave like a savage stallion and the mystery of what the Barrett family do in their house on hot afternoons. Number fifteen *Tamarisk Row,* green of a shade that has never been seen in Australia, orange of shadeless plains and pink of naked skin, for the hope of discovering something rare and enduring that sustains a man and his wife at the centre of what seem to be no more than stubborn plains where they spend long uneventful years waiting for the afternoon when they and the whole of a watching city see in the last few strides of a race what it was all for.

HELEN GARNER

1942-

HELEN GARNER HAS WORKED ACROSS A WIDE VARIETY OF
literary forms, winning awards for her fiction, non-fiction and
screenwriting. Garner burst on to the scene with her first novel
Monkey Grip (1977), set amongst the sharehouses of Carlton. In
the mid-1990s Garner seized the spotlight when her book *The First
Stone* (1995) investigated a high-profile case of sexual harass-
ment. More recently Garner has enjoyed success with *Joe Cinque's
Consolation* (2004), Garner's perspective on the true story of the
murder of Joe Cinque, and her novel *The Spare Room* (2008) won
both the Vance Palmer Prize for Fiction in the 2008 Victorian
Premier's Literary Awards and the Queensland Premier's Award
for Fiction 2008. In 2006 Garner won the inaugural Melbourne
Prize for Literature, acknowledging her body of work and her con-
tribution to Australian literature.

MONKEY GRIP

HELEN GARNER

MCPHEE GRIBBLE/PENGUIN BOOKS, RINGWOOD, 1991, P. 1

IN THE OLD BROWN HOUSE ON THE CORNER, A MILE FROM
the middle of the city, we ate bacon for breakfast every morning of our
lives. There were never enough chairs for us all to sit up at the meal
table; one or two of us always sat on the floor or on the kitchen step,
plate on knee. It never occurred to us to teach the children to eat with

a knife and fork. It was hunger and all sheer function: the noise, and clashing of plates, and people chewing with their mouths open, and talking, and laughing. Oh, I was happy then. At night our back yard smelt like the country.

It was early summer.

And everything, as it always does, began to heave and change.

It wasn't as if I didn't already have somebody to love. There was Martin, teetering as many were that summer on the dizzy edge of smack, but who was as much a part of our household as any outsider could be. He slept very still in my bed, jumped up with the kids in the early morning, bore with my crankiness and fits of wandering heart. But he went up north for a fortnight and idly, at the turning of the year, I fell in love with our friend Javo, the bludger, just back from getting off dope in Hobart: I looked at his burnt skin and scarred nose and violently blue eyes. We sat together in the theatre, Gracie on my knee. He put his hand to the back of my head. We looked at each other, and would have gone home together without a word being spoken ...

ALEX MILLER

1936–

INTRODUCTION AND EXTRACT CHOICE BY ROBIN GRIMWADE, READER

ALEX MILLER'S THIRD NOVEL, *THE ANCESTOR GAME* (1992), explores the question of identity and belonging, and how cultural traditions can influence such concepts. Do displacement, alienation and rejection destroy the individual's ability to feel 'at home', or is he always to feel exiled, 'severed from his tribe'? China and the cities of Shanghai and Hangzhou are central to these questions as they form. The Ancestor Game won numerous prizes for Miller, including the Miles Franklin Literary Award and the Commonwealth Writer's Prize.

THE ANCESTOR GAME

ALEX MILLER

ALLEN & UNWIN, ST LEONARDS, 2000, P. 259

DON'T BE AFRAID OF AUSTRALIA, THE DOCTOR HAD SAID TO HIM when they were walking together in the park one autumn afternoon, a day when the sky above Shanghai had been clear and blue and people had seemed to have all the time in the world to stroll and to feed the ducks and to sit and gaze into space. Long for something you can't name, the doctor said, and call it Australia. A thing will come into being. See a golden city on a plain, shining in the distance, and be certain the greatest prize existence can bestow on you is to belong somewhere among your own kind. Let it be Fairyland, an other-world. A land imagined and dreamed, not an actual place. The ancients of all nations understood that we don't belong anywhere real. They understood that the mystery of life, the paradox of our existence, is located in that charged space between the present reality of our individual life and the dream of the immortality of our species. It's the Phoenix, among the mythical beasts, which embodies this paradox for both the occidental and the oriental worlds alike.

PETER CAREY
1943–

INTRODUCTION AND EXTRACT CHOICE BY ROBYN ANNEAR, WRITER

PETER CAREY ENCOUNTERED NED KELLY'S JERILDERIE LETTER sometime in the mid-1960s. He copied out a portion and kept it in his wallet for years until, by close study or osmosis, the bushranger's 1879 manifesto—all raw and boiling, rat-charming Irish righteousness—seeped into Carey's bloodstream, with *True History of the Kelly Gang* (2000) the result. In the voice from the Jerilderie letter, brewed strong and brilliantly sustained, Carey's Ned addresses his own account of the 'Kelly outrage' to an infant daughter he will never meet. The novel won Carey his second Booker Prize and broadcast to the world one of Australian history's most lacerating episodes. The iron suit never mattered less than in Carey's telling of this foundational story, the man inside it never more.

TRUE HISTORY OF THE KELLY GANG

PETER CAREY

UNIVERSITY OF QUEENSLAND PRESS, ST LUCIA, 2000, PP. 372-3

JOE SAT DOWN HEAVILY UPON THE HURDLE HIS FACE SEIZED in his hands. O Jesus Ned he moaned I'm sick he looked up at me with his bloodshot eyes the icicles & frost was melting his beard were matted like a sorry dog.

Aaron sets out with the police tomorrow night.

Sets out for where?

He swayed so far back upon the hurdle I reached out to steady him but he chopped my hand angrily aside.

For here said he.

There was silence in the hut as we all saw what had occurred.

You done the right thing mate.

O I wish to God I were not your adjectival mate he cried I don't want what lies ahead.

Dan were sitting in front of the fire with his back to us but now he stood his bright eyes shining from his dirty face this were a boy no longer but a Kelly burnt and hardened by the fates.

Shut your hole he said you are our mate we won't let you suffer.

I seen the future said Joe every adjectival night I see the things that happen in my dreams.

It aint you thats going to suffer its effing Sherritt he's a dead man now.

You wouldnt understand you mongrel he's my mate he's trying to save my life.

Shutup I snapped at them I were the Captain and it were time to cease this endless bicker. Removing a piece of paper from my britches I

lay it before Joe's poisoned eyes.

What is it he asked and turned it upside down.

It is the pattern for the ironclad man.

Who is he asks Joe.

He is you said I he is a warrior he cannot die.

STEVEN CARROLL
1949–

INTRODUCTION AND EXTRACT CHOICE BY
PETER MARES, WRITER AND BROADCASTER

STEVEN CARROLL'S 'GLENROY NOVELS' CHRONICLE THE LIFE of a family in an emerging Melbourne suburb: Vic, a train driver who drinks too much; Rita, his disappointed wife; and their cricket-playing son Michael, who dreams of bowling the perfect delivery. The series begins in the 1950s with *The Art of the Engine Driver* (2001) moves into the 1960s with *The Gift of Speed* (2004) and lands in the 1970s with *The Time We Have Taken* (2007), which won the 2008 Miles Franklin Literary Award. (The first two novels were both shortlisted for the same prize in previous years). All three novels are deeply Australian, capturing the postwar boom in European migration, the social tensions and antagonisms of the Cold War, the incremental growth of women's independence and sexual liberation, the growing cult of the car and above all, the experience of life on the expanding suburban frontier in an era fuelled by the ideal of progress.

To read Carroll is to slow down, to adjust your perceptions and revel in the beauty of the everyday, the art of the ordinary, the 'sheer wonder of just being alive'.

THE ART OF THE ENGINE DRIVER

STEVEN CARROLL

HARPER PERENNIAL, PYMBLE, 2008, PP. 272–5

SOON THEY WILL ENTER THE HOUSE, ONE AT A TIME. AND WHEN they do it will be filled with the familiar silence that comes to a house when nobody's talking. For a few moments, as they walked along the street earlier that evening, as they paused by the long grass of the vacant paddocks, the night seemed to contain the promise that things would be different. But it was never going to be different. Michael knows that. It was always going to end like this.

It is then that he stops, stock-still on the footpath with his hands clenched by his side and looks about the street, glowering into that warm, boozy Saturday night, demanding more of the world, with all the ridiculous rage and anger of a powerless child. To his right, swaying slightly above the houses, are the tall pines of the school. A row of five pines, tall as the mills. One Saturday morning he climbed the tallest of those pines. For a quarter of an hour, branch by branch, feet wedged into the gaps of the tree's trunk for grip, he climbed the tree. Pausing on boughs as he did to regain his breath and strength in the hot summer air. But finally, he'd climbed as far as he could. There had been only a slight breeze on the ground, but the wind had been strong up there. He had gripped the branch that he sat on while the tree swayed from side to side. And sometimes, when the wind picked up, it almost seemed to topple forward as

if it were about to fall over onto the playground, the shelter shed and the red school buildings of the third and fourth grade classes below him.

He's standing in the street looking at the pines, and he can feel the bark under his palms, smell the sap, and feel the cool wind on his face while he sways from side to side as if he were perched on the lookout of a ship's mast. And from those remembered, windy heights of the pine tree he can still see the suburb spread out below him as it was that morning; the dirt roads, intersecting and crossing each other in the morning sun, the old settlers' homes in the distance, the shining, silver railway lines that divide the suburb between east and west, the railway station, the flour mills beside the station, the factory owner's four acre mansion to the right of the mills, his Bentley parked at the end of a long, sweeping driveway, the grazing cattle on the shrunken farm in front of him, the bluestone farmhouse, the old stable, the old wheat road, the war memorial, the shops, the black, bitumen line of the main street, the golf course, the greens and fairways, the square, box houses with their bare yards and struggling gardens, and the dry creek that trickles through it all.

And almost directly below him, his own street. From up there he could see into everybody's yards, see old man Malek watering his potatoes, Mr Younger staring at a partially completed wall of his house with a hammer in his hand, Mrs Bruchner in her garden chair, and just coming into view, his father, turning off the main road and cycling towards their street after having finished the night shift.

He'd never seen it all so completely before, the street, the whole suburb, spread out below him. He had hurried down the tree, sliding down the trunk, stopping occasionally at the boughs and branches, until he dropped back onto the pine-needle ground and began running, determined to beat his father back home.

Suddenly, standing in the street, his fists clenched tight, his knuckles white and his nails biting into the soft flesh of his palms. Suddenly, he wants that view again. And instead of continuing along the street as he normally would, he turns and begins running down the small lane that leads to the creek. To his father he would only have been a faint blur of movement in the night, vaguely recognisable as his child. As Michael hits the creek he leaps it, lands with a thud on the other side, and continues running along the lane until he reaches the tall pines of the schoolyard. And, walking to the tallest of those pines, he begins to climb.

CASTIGLIA &

SVAL

TERKIE

Vessel :- ....

Pass Name :- ....

Nominal Roll No. :- ....

Dormitory/Cabin :- ....

Berth No. :- ....

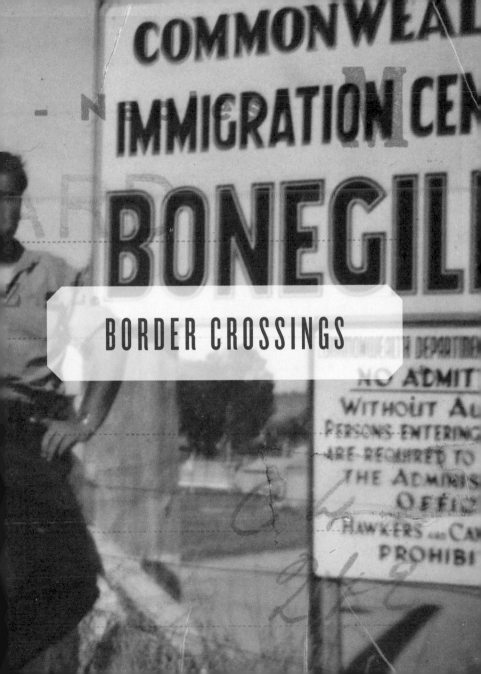

COMMONWEAL
IMMIGRATION CEN
BONEGILL

BORDER CROSSINGS

COMMONWEALTH DEPARTMENT
NO ADMIT
WITHOUT AU
PERSONS ENTERING
ARE REQUIRED TO
THE ADMINIS
OFFIC
HAWKERS and CA
PROHIBI

WRITERS FROM ALL CONTINENTS AND COUNTRIES have played a part in the formation of Australian literature. For the first century of Victoria's existence it was the literary work of Anglo-Australians that dominated our reading, but just as we celebrate this history it's vital to recognise the full range and effect of the various border crossings that have given life to our modern literature.

The major theme that's surfaced from all writers new to Australia has been the effect of having to navigate a new life in a new land. But the experience of writers from non-English-speaking backgrounds has involved significant other challenges. Such writers have been forced to face the dominance of Anglo-Celtic culture; they have had to make their way in a mostly mono-lingual country, dealing with the racism and eruptions that cultural clashes can bring. The literature that has evolved has enabled us to see into the inner lives of those that have been displaced and to compare, contrast and combine their experiences with those of the mainstream.

There is no one type of 'migrant literature', rather it has included a wide range of stories, styles and forms, including literature in translation, recollections and memoirs, and the fiction of those forced to make their way between two cultures. With each successive wave of migration the worldview of Australian experience has grown, and the grip of cultural insularity has been prised open.

We are truly part of the world and our writers are, more and more, engaging with ideas not solely the province of any one country. World wars, cheaper travel, a globalised economy and new technologies have all forced cultures to bend and meld. Ideas have been brought into a common market, so the work of many Australian writers — from all cultures — is now more inclined to contribute to a discussion that crosses borders.

Due to the significantly multicultural nature of Victoria, the experience of migration has driven a particular stream of Victorian writing. The 'literature of displacement' has developed into one of the strongest themes in Australian literature, and Victorians of all cultures have been at the forefront of this stream of writing. Our literature seems to have progressed to the point where the migrant search for 'home' has melded with the greater search for meaning in Australian life and an understanding of our place in the world.

HERZ BERGNER
1907–1970

INTRODUCTION AND EXTRACT CHOICE BY ARNOLD ZABLE, WRITER

BETWEEN SKY AND SEA WAS WRITTEN IN YIDDISH, IN MELBOURNE, during the latter stages of the Second World War. Herz Bergner had emigrated to Melbourne, from Warsaw, on the eve of war, in 1939. Translated into English by Judah Waten, the novella depicts the fate of traumatised Holocaust victims in search of refuge, en route to Australia, on board a Greek freighter. The passengers are trapped between sky and sea, and within the nightmares of their recent past. The passengers no longer know where they are, and still the ship drifts without any sight of land. The novella was well received by Australian critics and was awarded the 1946 Gold Medal of the Australian Literary Society. It was, possibly, the first Australian novel written in a language other than English that received mainstream recognition.

BETWEEN SKY AND SEA

HERZ BERGNER

TRANSLATED BY JL WATEN, DOLPHIN PUBLICATIONS,
MELBOURNE, 1946, PP. 11–13

FOR FIVE WEEKS THE DIRTY, OLD GREEK TRAMP STEAMER HAD drifted painfully over stormy waters without sighting land. She creaked with age as she allowed herself to be tossed by the green waves which played with her like young children tormenting a senile old man. It seemed as though the ship had lost its way and would forever trudge across the seas. Nothing had been seen but sky and sea and the people on deck were weary of gazing into the distance, hoping that a fragment of land would swim into their vision. They were now accustomed to the steely glare of the sun during the day when they could not keep their eyes open, and to blackness of night when they could not recognize each other. The order that no light was to be shown at night, not even a match was to be struck, had been given as soon as the ship sailed into the open sea.

On dark nights, when no moon shone, a solid tarry darkness surrounded the ship. She moved slowly like a black hearse and the Jews moved about aimlessly on the deck and the narrow, slippery, worn steps of the spiral staircase. In the darkness they groped blindly with their hands as they stumbled against each other, unable to find a resting place. Men looked for their wives and wives for their husbands. Children who had lost their mothers screamed in the black night and their frightened cries spread fear.

"Muma! Mu-ma! Where are you, Muma?"

Good friends who had talked for hours during the day passed each other like strangers. Suspiciously they allowed everybody to pass, recognizing friends only by their voices. A familiar voice brought warmth and friendliness and drew them together as if in a new-found joy.

"That's Fabyash, isn't it?" One man stopped another, touching him with his hands and peering at him short-sightedly.

"Am I right? Hah?"

"Yes, Yes, that's right. It's me, Fabyash. Why should a man be crawling around so late in the dark? It's too terrible to believe. You can feel the blackness with your hands."

Although the Captain had ordered them to stay in their cabins and to go to bed early, they could not stay still; every one was drawn outside. How could they go to sleep so early? From day to day things became worse. Overnight new orders were born. Pasted on the rotting, greasy walls of the boat, notices screamed in strange, big letters, crudely written. Then, one bright day, they found a new placard on the wall. It was cut from ordinary packing paper and still smelt of fresh ink, and it ordered that water was to be used only in an emergency for drinking purposes. Food had been supplied twice daily, but the dismal stew was shrinking from day to day, getting thinner and less plentiful. And the notices warned the crowd to remain quiet and not to become alarmed.

Instead of calming the passengers, these last words cast a shadow of fear, and people began to say that things must be bad. They won't admit how bad things are! The passengers purposely avoided the walls on which the notices were posted, afraid of new menaces. And in order to quieten their fears, uninvited, they began to creep into each other's cabins. They talked about the countries they had wandered through since they had been driven from their homes, and they outdid each other in knowledge of the new country for which they were bound—Australia. Although no one knew much, or had even heard much, about this new land, each one had a great deal to say about the country, its people and their customs …

Fabyash knew for certain that the country was surrounded by water on all sides and the people lived by catching fish, which they exported to the rest of the world. He was a small, energetic young man who always knew more than anyone else and nothing in the world could surprise him. He always knew everything in advance, and he had a bellyful of knowledge about Australia … But Zainval Rockman never could stand Fabyash's boastings and with a wave of the hand he rejected this infor-

mation. He was always looking for an excuse to show that Fabyash knew nothing and was nothing but a blatherskite. This time he really did talk Fabyash down and make him look small. He said that in the new country people lived by timber. The country is still wild and has plenty of forests, so the people export timber to the rest of the world …

Hearing this, Mrs. Hudess, a Warsaw woman, who was proud that she came from a big city, rose from her place. She said neither Fabyash nor Rockman knew what they were talking about. The country lives neither on fish nor timber. Australia is a country like any other country, with many big cities. Let Rockman and Fabyash stop talking nonsense and making Australia into a desert.

JUDAH WATEN

1911–1985

EXTRACT CHOICE BY DAVID CARTER, WRITER AND ACADEMIC

JUDAH WATEN WAS BORN IN ODESSA ON THE SHORES OF THE Black Sea and came to Australia with his family in 1925. Waten was a member of both the Communist Party of Australia and of the Realist Writers' Group, and he professed a desire to 'write about people I knew, real people as it were'. In *Alien Son* (1952), Waten brings together a series of loosely connected autobiographical stories to tell the tale of a young Jewish boy caught between two worlds: that of his school, where he is treated with disdain, and that of his home, where he finds the customs of his family foreign to him.

ALIEN SON

JUDAH WATEN

PICADOR/PAN MACMILLAN, SYDNEY, 1993, PP. 179–81

BUT SOON MOTHER WAS FILLED WITH MISGIVINGS. FATHER'S world, the world of commerce and speculation, of the buying and selling of goods neither seen nor touched, was repugnant and frightening to her. It lacked stability, it was devoid of ideals, it was fraught with ruin. Father was a trader in air, as the saying went.

Mother's anxiety grew as she observed more closely his mode of life. He worked in fits and starts. If he made enough in one hour to last him a week or a month his business was at an end and he went off in search of friends and pleasure. He would return to business only when his money had just about run out. He was concerned only with one day at a time; about tomorrow he would say, clicking his fingers, his blue eyes focused mellowly on space, 'We'll see.'

But always he had plans for making great fortunes. They never came to anything but frequently they produced unexpected results. It so happened that on a number of occasions someone Father trusted acted on the plans he had talked about so freely before he even had time to leave the tea-house. Then there were fiery scenes with his faithless friends. But Father's rage passed away quickly and he would often laugh and make jokes over the table about it the very same day. He imagined everyone else forgot as quickly as he did and he was always astonished to discover that his words uttered hastily in anger had made him enemies.

'How should I know that people have such long memories for hate? I've only a cat's memory,' he would explain innocently.

'If you spit upwards, you're bound to get it back in the face,' Mother irritably upbraided him.

Gradually Mother reached the conclusion that only migration to another country would bring about any real change in their life, and with all her persistence she began to urge him to take the decisive step. She considered America, France, Palestine, and finally decided on Australia. One reason for the choice was the presence there of distant relatives who would undoubtedly help them to find their feet in that far-away continent. Besides, she was sure that Australia was so different from any other country that Father was bound to acquire a new and more solid way of earning a living there.

For a long time Father paid no heed to her agitation and refused to make any move.

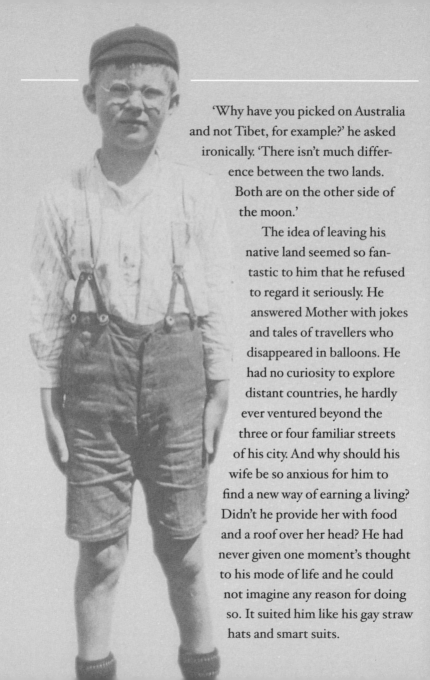

'Why have you picked on Australia and not Tibet, for example?' he asked ironically. 'There isn't much difference between the two lands. Both are on the other side of the moon.'

The idea of leaving his native land seemed so fantastic to him that he refused to regard it seriously. He answered Mother with jokes and tales of travellers who disappeared in balloons. He had no curiosity to explore distant countries, he hardly ever ventured beyond the three or four familiar streets of his city. And why should his wife be so anxious for him to find a new way of earning a living? Didn't he provide her with food and a roof over her head? He had never given one moment's thought to his mode of life and he could not imagine any reason for doing so. It suited him like his gay straw hats and smart suits.

Yet in the end he did what Mother wanted him to do, though even on the journey he was tortured by doubts and he positively shouted words of indecision. But he was no sooner in Australia than he put way all thoughts of his homeland and he began to regard the new country as his permanent home. It was not so different from what he had known before. Within a few days he had met some fellow merchants and, retiring to a café, they talked about business in the new land. There were fortunes to be made here, Father very quickly concluded. There was, of course, the question of a new language but that was no great obstacle to business. You could buy and sell — it was a good land, Father said.

It was different with Mother. Before she was one day off the ship she wanted to go back.

The impressions she gained on that first day remained with her all her life. It seemed to her there was an irritatingly superior air about the people she met, the customs officials, the cab men, the agent of the new house. Their faces expressed something ironical and sympathetic, something friendly and at the same time condescending. She imagined everyone on the wharf, in the street, looked at her in the same way and she never forgave them for treating her as if she were in need of their good-natured tolerance.

ΠΟ

1951–

INTRODUCTION AND EXTRACT CHOICE BY ARNOLD ZABLE, WRITER

24 HOURS IS AN EPIC POEM OF GREAT DARING, AN ACT OF HOMAGE to the working-class suburbs of inner Melbourne, particularly Fitzroy, where the author's father, a Greek immigrant, ran a cafe. ΠΟ, who was born in 1951, arrived in Melbourne with his family in 1954. As a writer, he has remained connected to his immigrant roots. In *24 Hours,* he conveys his readers and audience in and out of the cafes and snooker halls of Fitzroy, its pinball parlours and souvlaki bars, its takeaways, pubs, high-rise flats, milk bars, barber shops, laundrettes, fish and chip shops and factories, its back lanes and backrooms. As both a storyteller and performance poet, ΠΟ intends his work to be both proclaimed aloud and read on the written page. It reflects the poetry of everyday speech, the unique dialects of Greeks and Turks, ockers and Jugoslavs, of street people, and working people, struggling to move in from the margins and make ends meet. It plays on sounds and images, on syntax and dialect, and on what can be observed on the walls and streets.

24 HOURS

Π o

COLLECTIVE EFFORT PRESS, MELBOURNE, 1996, PP. 197-9

Balcha gives-Up
the fight, and goes over and sits down
    ... at the Table.
He tells Bobbie (an' the
    kid) : Grik o'rayt!
Thai brring "Sivilayzaishon"/Filosofi
    ...... itz'etrra, but
thai STUK!
    Yoogoslaavia iz a RICH!
Thai hev tha "miniraalz" en thingz.
    Grik ... duzen hev!
Dai itting STONZ! N-o hev graas!
    Kunn progressing!
Wit "Wun Dolla" yoo ken paas AWL dai!
    Yoo kennot CHAYNJ da Draahkma!, he sez:
Dai n-o LETTING!

    Robert sez: he
went back (to Yugo) for a visit
    .... 5 years ago.
One night, he got "drunk" and started
    looking for the T.A.B.
They didn't have one!
    He couldn't get used to the Life-style.

He had a few drinks, and they
    wouldn't take
his Traveller's cheques.
    Lucky there was a bloke there
who understood him, he said.
    He asked him, what kind they were?
"Kangaroo-Dollars", he said, and
the bloke started
                                    "laughing".

    Balcha sez:
he told Foti (over at the
    other Club) if he ever wins Tattslotto
he's going to take him to Europe
    but, not Greece (:cos
they haven't got Taxis there (at the
    Airport) only Donkeys!.

    The bloke (sitting down
next to Balcha) sez, he was 17 when he
    .... 1st came to Australia.
He lived in a bungalo (at the back
    of a house) in Footscray.
It was under a tree.
    He was paying $10 a week.
And working everyday. -No electricity! -
    On weekends, he sez
he used to "walk" to Yarraville, and back,

in the dark.
Upto a Greek club!
     T-o s-o … "kooraasi" (ikinnes
tis merres) then t-o pistevva!
     Thoolya/Spiti
                                   Thoolya/Spiti
k e na e-rhhotaan-e e'nnas "visitaas"
     e' .k.l.i.n.a.
tin borrta, sun THEN ton
     aa'koo-ggha!

     It was a different World then!
The magpies used to swoop-Down at you
     … layk, Stootka!
and if you
lived in a Boarding-House, and
a Woman came over to visit
you had to keep the bedroom-door Open, or
the Landlady would come over
and knock on the door
cos she didn't want to turn it
into a "Brothel", a bloke sez.

     Balcha sez:
He was so,ooo "poor" then, all he
     could afford to eat
was DOG FOOD!

He use to add abit of "onion" to it,
to give it abit of flavour, and
    on Friday's
he'd ... switch-over to
    CAT FOOD!

    Don't ...
listen to him!, a bloke sez:
    Evribodi hev
tha "maynaasez" en "plaasez" - Don TAYK
    onli tha Wun!
Aastraalia (for ... mi), (en US), was
    Gol'-mayn!!!

Thet taym
if yoo finish for tha munni,
    evribodi poot HEN in da poket to
giv YOO! - En if, yoo n-o get
off him hee get

                    UFFTendet!

The Boss
.... comes round (wiping the Tables).
    Good kuntri.
Good kuntri! he sez, but iz hev
    styoopet-pipol!
Klevva-pipol GON EWT for dis playc!
    Only tha "Styoopet"

                    hee-a!

ANIA WALWICZ

1951–

INTRODUCTION AND EXTRACT CHOICE BY JUDITH RODRIGUEZ,
POET, ACADEMIC AND EDITOR

ANIA WALWICZ CAME TO AUSTRALIA FROM POLAND IN 1963.
Associative tours de force, her short prose pieces enact the mis-
understandings, dislocations, and anxieties of (for instance)
growing up, migration and the life of a large city. Her books are
writing (1982), *boat* (1989), and a mother-memoir *red roses*

(1992). Fellow writer Steven Carroll describes her writing as: 'The open text which proposes the notion of serious game playing at the heart of postmodernist writing . . .'

BOAT

ANIA WALWICZ

SIRIUS/ANGUS & ROBERSTON PUBLISHERS, NORTH RYDE, 1989, PP. 81–2

land lord

pipe burst call mister plumber he come greek landlord mister next door please come in he tell call greek plumber come they look come go hello go for a look go back yard have see what talk greek i don't understand a word don't understand a word what did come again tell me please he he he landlord is tell me what fix did the greek plumber greek landlord come in to my kitchen he tell me tell he forgot you know how what when forget when you forget switch wave length landlord he the mister next door talk to me talk to me he greek forgets that me that i don't that i can't greek speak no understan see but he he he landlord greek talks greek to me just a slip a mistake error funny sorry embarrassed he greek to me sounds are words to look at me look at me landlord greek greek talks to me greek in i can't see tell me what happens what the plumber said what did happen little sounds out of his mouth bubble says come to me tell me every thing what plumber pipe burst told landlord pipe burst told me landlord what about the pipe what about the washer what about my plumbing the connecting all joining what about everything don't want to live with my parents landlord says by mistake just an error he forgot how to hear some one foreign tongue tried to make sounds he made me scared i was scared this is greek to me what's going on try to pretend that nothing happened really just an error you know a slip can happen anyone called teacher mummy once everyone laughed said wrong words are only bleeps are sounds he he he landlord greek talks greek to me try to listen don't laugh at me keep a straight face save and save he burst pipe tells me what my plumber said to me his tongue doesn't belong don't make these words don't belong to me what is what what nobody understand a knot baby plumber greek my parents talk else what mister landlord tells me words that are somewhere else just a slip a mistake won't happen again promise just bit nervous see got him worried just a breakdown minute phone went dead beep a call line block landlord face greek my mouth makes words a ooo beee bee boo a zee zee zee is bicycle a bicycle a lamp lamp lamp how do you know what i think how do you know what i now think

ARNOLD ZABLE

1947-

ARNOLD ZABLE IS A STORYTELLER WHO HAS USED HIS SKILLS as a novelist, journalist and performer to marry the past with the present. He weaves fact and fiction together to give voice and meaning to the stories of migrants and locals alike. Zable's first book, *Jewels and Ashes* (1991), was an autobiographical novel that won five Australian awards; his second, *Cafe Scheherazade* (2001), unites the accounts of Holocaust survivors as told to him in the St Kilda cafe of the same name. Zable has often written

about and advocated for the plight of refugees and is currently
the president of the Melbourne chapter of International PEN,
the worldwide association of writers that fights for freedom of
expression.

CAFE SCHEHERAZADE

ARNOLD ZABLE

TEXT PUBLISHING, MELBOURNE, 2001, PP. 150–3

WALK THE FAMILIAR ROUTE. THE INNER CITY IS COATED IN DEW.
St Kilda pier is lined with lamps that glow like miniature moons. A
woman leans across the rails. A couple embrace on the deserted beach,
a middle-aged man slumps back on a wooden seat. The Palais Theatre
rears like a Gothic castle in the mist.

Walk the streets of Shanghai; walk the lanes of Krochmalna; walk the
crumbling courtyards of Vilna; the foothills of Kobe; walk the ancient
trading route. Walk the pier. Walk the pavement. Walk the shoreline of
the bay. Walk and come to know that others have walked here for mil-
lennia. Walk the contours, the flatlands, the hills, the rivers and creeks
coursing like arteries to the bay. Walk and come to know that this land
abounds in tales, both ancient and new.

Retrace your steps along the familiar route. Observe the neon sign
coming into view, Scheherazade blinking lilac, pink and blue. Proceed
through the glass doors. Make your way past the front alcove where the
boys are playing cards. Move past the men immersed in journals and
racing guides. Sidestep the tables where families are gulping down their
meals; and make your way to the back room.

They are there, as usual, Mr and Mrs Zeleznikow, Avram and Masha, the proprietors, in their directors' chairs, issuing orders, poring over bills, shuffling papers, reading the news.

So join us, dear reader. Don't be shy. Here, have a slice of Black Forest cake. On the house. And a glass of red. Savour it. Feel the glow spreading over your cheeks. Allow the taste to linger in the mouth. It is a pleasant feeling, no? Are you comfortable? Sit back. Settle into your chair; and listen to *bobbe mayses*, grandma tales:

> Listen to this story children,
> Listen with nose and eyes.
> Over grandma's house
> A cow I saw did fly.
> This is true, this is true,
> This is true, it all took place.
> This is true, this is true,
> This indeed, I saw myself.

The war is over. Empires lie in ruins. A weariness has descended upon the world. Travellers trudge across the horizon clad in rags. They sleep in barns, abandoned cottages, burnt-out buildings. They emerge from temporary refuges, remote hamlets. They disperse from disbanding armies and the labour camps of the east. It is time to seek out the loved ones they have left behind. It is time to journey home.

Masha's family were among the first to return to Poland. In September 1945, the Frydmans boarded a train in Dzhambul. Cold winds penetrated the wagons. The early snows were falling. Tall grasses bent to a bitter breeze. Forests vanished into the shadows. Villages receded in huddles of light.

SCHEHEREZADE ← Restaurant COFFEE LOUNGE

They travelled in silence. All about them they saw others on the move; on the backs of trucks, in bare feet, on bicycles and horse-drawn carts; they moved like weary battalions in quiet retreat. They travelled towards a land shrouded in rumours. They prayed that their loved ones had survived. They were afraid of what they would find.

Yet nothing could have prepared them for the devastation that had been wrought in their absence: the piles of rubble, twisted girders, the razed hamlets, the wastelands of defeat. Nothing could have readied them for the scorched earth, the ruined cities, the desecrated temples and shattered homes.

This is when their stories began to be suppressed. This is when the Frydmans, and so many others who had survived in the east, were overwhelmed by the demands of others in far greater distress; and by an urgent need to forget, to bury the past and to rebuild their aborted lives.

CHRISTOS TSIOLKAS

1965-

INTRODUCTION AND EXTRACT CHOICE BY JO CASE, WRITER AND EDITOR

CHRISTOS TSIOLKAS BURST ONTO THE AUSTRALIAN LITERARY scene in 1994 with his much-praised debut novel *Loaded*. Due to his raw, confrontational prose style, steeped in sex and drugs, he was initially branded as part of the 'grunge' literary movement of the 1990s, then at its height. His third novel, *Dead Europe* (2005), a vibrant novel of ideas, took him six years to write. It explores— among other things—racism (particularly anti-Semitism) and what has happened to European peasant culture as it was 'brought screeching and howling into the modern age'. It won the *Age* Fiction Book of the Year Award 2006 and the 2006 Melbourne Prize for Literature in the category of best writer under forty. His latest book, *The Slap* (2008), won the Best Book award at the 2009 Commonwealth Writers' Awards.

DEAD EUROPE

CHRISTOS TSIOLKAS

VINTAGE/RANDOM HOUSE, MILSONS POINT, 2005, PP. 81–4

GIULIA HAD CHANGED. GONE WERE THE BAGGY DENIM JACKETS and jeans of a Communist Party cadre, replaced now by a thin silk shirt that revealed her cleavage. Her hair had been cut short and thick gold hoop earrings helped accentuate the angularity of her cheekbones and jaw. She was truly a beautiful woman but age was beginning to creep in: wrinkles, shadows and lines beneath her eyes. But her conversation with Andreas was furious and sophisticated, and reminded me a little of my previous shame all those years ago to be the naive traveller from the bottom of the earth. Andreas too worked for television, a journalist who nonchalantly mentioned his time in Sarajevo, Belgrade and Istanbul, which, in the Greek manner, he insisted on calling Constantinopoli. Giulia too had covered the earthquakes in that city and I listened fascinated to their stories. Andreas asked me questions about my profession and I found myself bullshitting, pretending that my photographic career was far more successful than it was, not mentioning the weekend job in the video shop I still had to make ends meet. Giulia looked on proudly.

—Of course, she insisted to Andreas, my cousin is a success. We are a noble family. She squeezed my fingers tightly and kissed my brow. Then taking my hand she opened it and deposited a gift. A small joint and a coarse yellow tablet lay in my palm. Her loud laughter rang through the square like church bells.

—The E's direct from Amsterdam, we have Andreas to thank for that.

Andreas bowed his head and smiled at me.

—I prefer my Ecstasy from Holland, he explained. People swear by London and Barcelona but in my experience that is not the case at all. I think it is Amsterdam for LSD and for Ecstasy.

—And for hashish?

Andreas smiled wickedly at Giulia's question.

—Ah, hashish is best when it is directly received from the hands of a young Pakistani peasant boy.

I placed the tablet and joint in my pocket and pretended a worldliness I did not feel. They were confusing me. They obviously had money, obviously were doing well, but their conversation was bitter and cynical. Giulia's mobile phone went off during our meal and she spoke rapidly and impatiently. I looked around the square and it hit me that from table to table, dinners, dates, conversations were being interrupted by the persistent clamour of the ringing phones. Giulia switched off her phone and turned to Andreas.

—Now you will suffer, that was Antoni. He has a room for me in High Street, Kensington. Serves you right.

Andreas again arched those long slim eyebrows.

—My Giuliana, how many times must I tell you? I detest London. It is a cold, foolish city.

—Bah! Noticing that I was distracted, Giulia turned to me and again took my hand. I am sorry, my little one, we are boring you with our terrible bourgeois conversation, all about work and silly things like that. I want to hear about you. She was searching my face, looking straight at my eyes. How is Colin? Why is he not here with you?

I tried to explain how Colin was a man uncomfortable with formality and artifice, who wanted a holiday to be time spent lounging on beaches or walking through rainforests, who detested the thought of openings, of exhibitions. My jumbled Greek sounded silly. I turned to Andreas and stated simply, in English, My boyfriend hates artists.

—A wise man.

Giulia crossed her arms in exasperation.

—He wouldn't have had to hang around fucking artists, I would have taken him places. Tell him, tell him that I very much want to meet Colin, the man who has stolen my cousin's heart.

I grinned and nodded.

—Maybe I will visit you both in Australia? Maybe I will come and live there? Yes, she insisted, I will come and live in the desert. I will take an Aboriginal man for a husband. I am bored with Europeans.

Andreas laughed at this.

—You would suffocate if you left Europe. You need this oxygen to survive. Leave the poor Australian men alone, marry a Greek, as your mother insists.

—I don't want to marry an Australian, exclaimed Giulia disdainfully. I said I will marry an old wise Aboriginal man.

—The only true Australians, I interceded.

Giulia's eyes flashed approvingly. Good, she answered, so you have finally realised you are a Greek?

I laughed and shook my head.

Giulia pointed at me and sneered.

—He keeps insisting he is not Greek, he is Australian.

Andreas looked at me and then laughed.

—That's preposterous. You are indeed a Greek. Not only physically but in your soul.

I protested that I did not grow up here, that I could not pretend to be anything but antipodean. They both looked at me strangely, then Giulia shrugged her shoulders and picked up her handbag. I fingered the tablet in my shirt pocket, eager for the heightening that drugs would bring to this singular summer night. Giulia smiled at me.

—We have surprise for you.

—What is it?

She glanced at her watch

—Time we had our sweets. Giulia slid the yellow pill onto her tongue, winked at me, and leaned over and kissed me. Andreas asked for the bill, and when it arrived he slapped my hand away and placed one hundred euros on the table. You are my guest tonight, he told me, interrupting my protests. I am paying for the Australian.

T.G.42B.

Sch. C. 4163
7/1943.

This Telegram has been received subject to the Post and Telegraph Act and Regulations. The time received at this office is shown at the end of the message.

CO

POST

Office of Origin.

No. of W

U 294 ADELAIDE STOCK EXCHANGE

JOHN REED

360 COLLINS STREET MELBOURNE

STRONG CHANCE MALLEY FRAUD HA

WILL YOU PHONE AFTER NINE

(360 MALLEY FRAUD)

WEALTH OF AUSTRALIA.

GENERAL'S DEPARTMENT.

EGRAM

The date stamp indicates
the date of reception and
lodgment also, unless an
earlier date is shown after
the time of lodgment

Time of Lodgment.

-30 A

POETS' CORNER

TECTIGE AGENCY INVESTIGATING

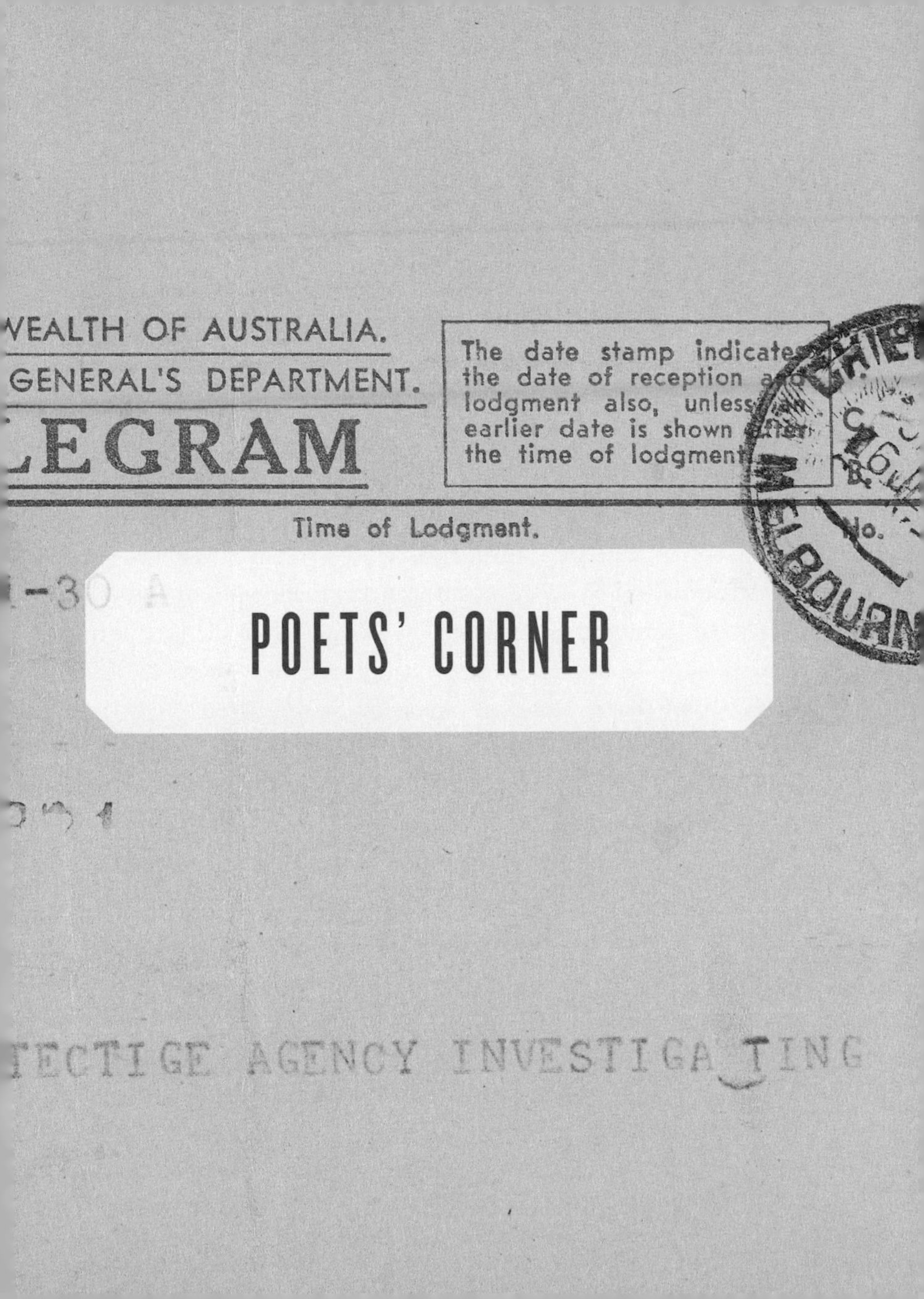

MOST NINETEENTH-CENTURY AUSTRALIAN POETRY was dominated by poems of natural reflection, doggerel, ballads and other songs adapted from British tunes. But in the years leading up to Federation, Australian poetry began to find a voice that was more at home in the newly forged nation.

At the beginning of the twentieth century humorous and vernacular poems held sway alongside the lyrical, and among those that espoused a nationalist vision. The horrors of the First World War drove many poets to ground their poetry in the reality of life and yet others sought to return to the classicism of earlier times.

Debate exists as to when modernism first found a place in Australian poetry, but Furnley Maurice (aka Frank Wilmot, from Victoria), writing from the 1920s to the 1940s, can probably claim to be one of Australia's earliest modernists, alongside Kenneth Slessor (from New South Wales). But these early adopters didn't quicken the pace of Australian modernism, and the slow uptake of modernist poetic principles was stalled further by the Ern Malley hoax. It wasn't until the cultural eruptions later in the 1960s that modernism became more fashionable.

The early 1960s were a time when Vincent Buckley and his editorship of the *Bulletin* reshaped Australian poetry away from the dominant bush themes that Douglas Stewart (the previous editor) had cultivated. In this period the intellectual tradition of Melbourne was described by Chris Wallace-Crabbe as 'reformist, socially critical, pro-union and historically nationalist'. However, the profusion of outlets for publication assisted the development of poetry across a broad spectrum, and the support of journals like *Meanjin* and *Overland*—in addition to the numerous 'little magazines' that flourished during this period—cannot be underestimated.

The economic boom of the postwar period provided more people with opportunities for higher education, and this had significant effects on the poetry of the period. The growth of university courses supported a growth in the intellectual aesthetics of modernism and postmodernism, and this remained the predominant force in poetry for some time, although there have been various reactions to this supremacy.

When Betty Burstall opened the La Mama theatre in 1967, she did so to support new work by both playwrights and poets. By taking poetry readings out of the universities, a new range of poets were able to publish their work through performance. This kind of poetry revelled in the immediacy of the connection of the poet with the audience and gave rise to the performance poetry scene.

As well as bringing economic prosperity, the postwar culture—and especially that of the 1960s—enhanced the international context of Victorian poets. Coupled with the coming of age of many poets—either born to migrant families or having migrated to Australia themselves—there was a far more pluralistic understanding of what gave life to our culture, and this was reflected in the huge range of poets and poems on offer.

Let your voice be
    delicate:
The bees are home:
All their days love
    is sunken
Safe in the comb.

John Shaw Neilson

JOHN SHAW NEILSON
1872-1942

INTRODUCTION AND EXTRACT CHOICE BY
TOBY DAVIDSON, POET, ACADEMIC AND REVIEWER

JOHN SHAW NEILSON MOVED TO THE WIMMERA–MALLEE region of north-west Victoria at a young age. The skies, birds, trees and the vast silences of the region captured his imagination as his writing skills were honed by his poet father and austere Presbyterian mother. When Neilson found fame through the *Bulletin* and his first collection *Heart of Spring* (1919), the popular myth of a simple, whimsical labourer who had somehow stumbled upon intimations of holiness proved remarkably resilient, enduring until the 1990s. The 2001 publication of Neilson's letters, by contrast, reveals a highly literary, well-read poet plagued by hardship and self-doubt who found consolation in rhymes about girls, birds and trees as spiritual intermediaries. From 1928 Neilson lived in Depression-era Melbourne, writing poems about the graces of everyday people amid the clatter of 'Stony Town'. Neilson's continuing popularity owes as much to his range as it does to his innate conservationism and eco-poetics, well before such terms existed. Ultimately, though, it is Neilson's musicality that captures and soothes his readers.

THE COLLECTED VERSE
A VARIORUM EDITION
JOHN SHAW NEILSON

AUSTRALIAN SCHOLARLY EDITIONS CENTRE,
UNSW AT ADFA, CANBERRA, 2003, PP. 779–81

Stony Town

If ever I go to Stony Town
I'll go as to a fair,
With bells and men and a dance girl
With a heat-wave in her hair.

I'll ask the birds that be on the road –
I dream (though it may not be)
That the eldest Song was a forest thought
And the Singer was a tree.

Oh, Stony Town is a hard town,
It buys and sells and buys;
It will not pity the plight of youth
Nor any Love in the eyes.

No curve they follow in Stony Town,
But the straight line and the square,
But the girl will dance them a royal dance
Like a blue wren at his prayer.

If ever I go to Stony Town
I'll go as to a fair,
And the girl shall shake with the cinnamon dust
And the heat-wave in her hair.

CJ DENNIS
1876–1938

INTRODUCTION AND EXTRACT CHOICE BY ∏O, POET

CJ DENNIS WAS THE POET OF *THE SENTIMENTAL BLOKE*. BY 1976, over 285,000 copies had been printed and sold worldwide. The pocket edition had been distributed to the Australian troops during the First World War. He wrote in the vernacular, declaring that if 'slang is the illegitimate sister of poetry, and if an illegitimate relationship is the nearest I can get I am content'. He created perhaps the most enduring characters in Australian literature: the Bloke, Ginger Mick, Digger Smith, Doreen and Rose of Spadgers Lane. His poems have been translated into a silent movie, a talkie, a stage play and a musical, as well as various radio, television and record/gramaphone productions. He worked as a freelance reporter, contributor, and as an editor for a number of newspapers including the *Bulletin*, the *Herald and Weekly Times*, the *Australian Worker*, and the *Call*. He lived and died at Toolangi, about 72 kilometres north-east of Melbourne.

SELECTED VERSE OF CJ DENNIS

CJ DENNIS

ANGUS & ROBERTSON, SYDNEY, 1950, PP. 18–19

The Play

"Wot's in a name?" she sez ... And then she sighs,
An' clasps 'er little 'ands, an' rolls 'er eyes.
"A rose," she sez, "be any other name
Would smell the same.
Oh, w'erefore art you, Romeo, young sir?
Chuck yer ole pot, an' change yer moniker!"

Doreen an' me, we bin to see a show—
The swell two-dollar touch. Bong tong, yeh know
A chair apiece wiv velvit on the seat;
A slap-up treat.
The drarmer's writ be Shakespeare, years ago,
About a barmy goat called Romeo.

"Lady, be yonder moon I swear!" sez 'e.
An' then 'e climbs up on the balkiney;
An' there they smooge a treat, wiv pretty words,
Like two love-birds.
I nudge Doreen. She whispers, "Ain't it grand!"
'Er eyes is shinin'; an' I squeeze 'er 'and.

"Wot's in a name?" she sez. 'Struth, I dunno.
Billo is just as good as Romeo.
She may be Juli-er or Juli-et—
'E loves 'er yet.
If she's the tart 'e wants, then she's 'is queen.
Names never count … But ar, I like "Doreen!"

A sweeter, dearer sound I never 'eard;
Ther's music 'angs around that little word,
Doreen! … But wot was this I starts to say
About the play?
I'm off me beat. But when a bloke's in love
'Is thorts turn 'er way, like a 'omin' dove.

This Romeo, 'e's lurkin' wiv a crew—
A dead tough crowd o' crooks—called Montague.
'Is cliner's push—wot's nicknamed Capulet—
They 'as 'em set.
Fair narks they are, jist like them back-street clicks,
Ixcep' they fights wiv skewers 'stid o' bricks.

Wot's in a name? Wot's in a string o' words?
They scraps in ole Verona wiv the'r swords,
An' never give a bloke a stray dog's chance,
An' that's Romance.
But when they deals it out wiv bricks an' boots
In Little Lon., they're low, degraded broots.

Wot's jist plain stoush wiv us, right 'ere to-day,
Is "valler" if yer fur enough away.
Some time, some writer bloke will do the trick
Wiv Ginger Mick,
Of Spadger's Lane. *'E'll* be a Romeo,
When 'e's been dead five 'undred years or so.

ERN MALLEY
1918-1943

INTRODUCTION AND EXTRACT CHOICE BY ΠO, POET

ERNEST LALOR MALLEY WAS BORN IN ENGLAND IN 1918 AND AFTER his father died (two years later), migrated to Australia. His mother died when he was fifteen, and his sister Ethel took care of him. He worked as a garage mechanic, insurance salesman and watch repairer. After his death of Grave's disease, Ethel found some poems of his and sent them in to the avant-garde journal *Angry Penguins*, edited by Max Harris. They were accepted and published in 1945. At this point the hoax was exposed—neither Ern Malley nor his sister Ethel existed in real life. It turned out that two soldiers (Lieutenant James McAuley and Corporal Harold Stewart) concocted the poems as a nonsense one lazy October Saturday, and sent them in under the name of the invented Ethel Malley. The hoax achieved world attention for a while, and modernism (once again) became a laughing stock. To add insult to injury, Max Harris was charged with publishing obscenity and

So Long

The wind masters the waves
As the waves the sea
And all of it ~~whole~~ entire
And none of it to me.

I had thought it was finished
~~And it is no use~~ And now it is useless
Like the writing on graves
Empty of future

Renew ~~the sign~~

the sign

At the moment of

taken to court. He was fined £5 or twelve weeks in jail, and the edition impounded. Max Harris maintained to his dying day that the 'nonsense' *was* nevertheless poetry.

THE DARKENING ECLIPTIC

ERN MALLEY

REED & HARRIS, MELBOURNE, 1944, PP. 17–18

Sonnets for the Novachord

(i.)

Rise from the wrist, o kestrel
Mind, to a clear expanse.
Perform your high dance
On the clouds of ancestral
Duty. Hawk at the wraith
Of remembered emotions.
Vindicate our high notions
Of a new and pitiless faith.
It is not without risk!
In a lofty attempt
The fool makes a brisk
Tumble. Rightly contempt
Rewards the cloud-foot unwary
Who falls to the prairie.

(ii.)

Poetry: the loaves and fishes,
Or no less miracle;
For in this deft pentacle
We imprison our wishes.

Though stilled to alabaster
This Ichthys shall swim
From the mind's disaster
On the volatile hymn.

If this be the norm
Of our serious frolic
There's no remorse:

Our magical force
Cleaves the ignorant storm
On the hyperbolic.

VINCENT BUCKLEY
1925-1988

INTRODUCTION AND EXTRACT CHOICE BY JAMIE GRANT, POET AND EDITOR

VINCENT BUCKLEY WAS BORN IN ROMSEY, VICTORIA, IN 1925 and was educated at Melbourne's St Patrick's College and Melbourne University. After further study at Cambridge University he joined the staff of Melbourne University, becoming Lockie Fellow in creative writing for three years from 1958, and being awarded a personal chair in 1967. From the late 1950s until the early 1970s Buckley was the most influential figure in a group of poets, all with connections to Melbourne University, who came to dominate the Australian poetry scene in the early 1960s. Buckley's best work is redolent of the biblical rhythms of his Catholic upbringing, as well as of the Irish accents of his ancestry. It is also rich in sense of place, particularly in his epic-length sequence *Golden Builders*, set in Melbourne's inner suburbs.

COLLECTED POEMS
VINCENT BUCKLEY

EDITED BY CHRIS WALLACE-CRABBE,
JOHN LEONARD PRESS, ELWOOD, 2009, P. 153

Golden Builders

I

The hammers of iron glow down Faraday.
Lygon and Drummond shift under their resonance.

Saws and hammers drawn across the bending air
shuttling like a bow; the saw trembles
the hammers are molten, they flow with quick light
striking; the flush spreads and deepens on the stone.
The drills call the streets together
stretching hall to lecture-room to hospital.

But prop old walls with battens of old wood.

Saturday work. Sabbath work. *On this day*
we laid this stone
to open this Sabbath School. Feed My Lambs.

The sun dies half-glowing in the floating brickdust,
suspended between red and saffron.
The colours resonate like a noise; the muscles of mouth
neck shoulders loins arm themselves against it.
Pavements clink like steel; the air soft,
palpable as cork, lets the stone cornices
gasp into it. Pelham surrenders, Grattan
runs leading forward, seeking the garden's breadth, the fearful
edge of green on which the sexes lay.

We have built this Sabbath School. Feed My Lambs.

Evening wanders through my hands and feet
my mouth is cool as the air that now thins

twitching the lights on down winding paths. Everything
leans on this bright cold. In gaps of lanes, in tingling
shabby squares, I hear the crying of the machines.

O Cardigan, Queensberry, Elgin: names of their lordships.
Cardigan, Elgin, Lygon: Shall I find here my Lord's grave?

BRUCE DAWE
1930–

INTRODUCTION AND EXTRACT CHOICE BY
CHRIS WALLACE-CRABBE, POET AND ESSAYIST

BORN IN GEELONG IN 1930, DONALD BRUCE DAWE SPENT
most of the 1950s in Melbourne, where he had many casual jobs
and was a transient but popular student with many on-campus
friends. Later, he served in the RAAF, completed a degree in
southern Queensland, where he has lived ever since, teaching lit-
erature until his retirement. Dawe has probably been the inventor
of middle-suburbia in Australian poetry. Unlike his sardonic near
contemporary, Barry Humphries, he has observed and treated our
common lives gently. Ever the droll moralist, he has long been a
keen observer of day-to-day mores.

SOMETIMES GLADNESS
COLLECTED POEMS 1954 TO 2005
BRUCE DAWE

PEARSON AUSTRALIA, MELBOURNE, 2006, PP. 86–7

Life-cycle
for Dig Jim Phelan

When children are born in Victoria
they are wrapped in the club-colours, laid in beribboned cots,
having already begun a lifetime's barracking.

Carn, they cry, Carn ... feebly at first
while parents playfully tussle with them
for possession of a rusk: Ah, he's a little Tiger! (And they are ...)

Hoisted shoulder-high at their first League game
they arc like innocent monsters who have been years swimming
towards the daylight's roaring empyrean

Until, now, hearts shrapnelled with rapture,
they break surface and are forever lost,
their minds rippling out like streamers

In the pure flood of sound, they are scarfed with light, a voice
like the voice of God booms from the stands
Ooohh you bludger and the covenant is sealed.
Hot pies and potato-crisps they will eat,

they will forswear the Demons, cling to the Saints
and behold their team going up the ladder into Heaven,

And the tides of life will be the tides of the home-team's fortunes
— the reckless proposal after the one-point win,
the wedding and honeymoon after the grand-final …

They will not grow old as those from more northern States grow old,
for them it will always be three-quarter-time
with the scores level and the wind advantage in the final term,

That passion persisting, like a race-memory, through the welter
　　of seasons,
enabling old-timers by boundary-fences to dream of resurgent lions
and centaur-figures from the past to replenish continually the present,

So that mythology may be perpetually renewed
and Chicken Smallhorn return like the maize-god
in a thousand shapes, the dancers changing

But the dance forever the same — the elderly still
loyally crying Carn … Carn … (if feebly) unto the very end,
having seen in the six-foot recruit from Eaglehawk their hope
　　of salvation.

CHRIS WALLACE-CRABBE
1934-

INTRODUCTION AND EXTRACT CHOICE BY
DAVID McCOOEY, POET, CRITIC AND ACADEMIC

CHRIS WALLACE-CRABBE, PROFESSOR EMERITUS AT MELBOURNE University, is best known for his poetry, but he is also an important critic and anthologist. In addition to his long academic career in Australia, he has also held fellowships and professorships abroad and his poetry has a significant international reputation. While strongly attracted to the Australian vernacular, the comic and the quotidian, Wallace-Crabbe's poetry also contains more sombre metaphysical concerns (seen especially in his elegies for his adult son).

SELECTED POEMS 1956-1994
CHRIS WALLACE-CRABBE
OXFORD UNIVERSITY PRESS, OXFORD, 1995, P. 10

The Swing

On a swing at midnight in the black park. Between poplars which are towers of light for a hidden street lamp and inky she oaks my arc is maintained. From lighter to darker I go, from dark to light; but only, as ever, to return.

Here we live in the imperfect syntax of light and darkness; wanting to write a sentence as perfect as the letter o in praise of things. For things exist supremely; all our values cohere in things.

The austere prose which could outline the world with a physicist's clarity never arrives. We move through the fugal elaboration of leaves, through centuries of drowning flowers. Unsatisfied, uncertain, I am swinging again tonight in the park.

KEVIN HART
1954–

INTRODUCTION AND EXTRACT CHOICE BY
PAUL MITCHELL, POET AND WRITER

KEVIN HART WAS BORN IN ENGLAND IN 1954, MIGRATING to Australia when he was eleven. He was brought up in Brisbane and later moved to Melbourne where he was for many years professor of English and comparative literature at Monash University. Hart now lives in the US and teaches at the University of Virginia. His poetry is known both for its romantic sensibilities and religious themes (raised a nominal Anglican, Hart converted to Catholicism in 1980). His collections include *Your Shadow* (1984), *Peniel* (1991), *Wicked Heat* (1999) and *Young Rain* (2008). Hart is also widely regarded as a philosopher, critic, theologian and translator, with works including *The Trespass of the Sign* (1989), *AD Hope* (1992) and the translation *The Buried Harbour: Selected Poems of Giuseppe Ungaretti*.

FLAME TREE
SELECTED POEMS
KEVIN HART

PAPER BARK PRESS, SYDNEY, 2002, P. 46

Your Shadow

Fed by its eye, the falcon
Swims with the flooding wind, watching
Its shadow writhe
Like something left half-dead.

Open your hand
And see the darkness nursed there; see how
Your shadow blossoms,
Your body's very own black flower.

It is a gift, a birth right, your baby shawl
Now growing into a shroud;
You are an eye, intent upon this world,
It is your pupil, shining.

Come closer, it is a trap-door
Into the secret earth, and one day soon
You will go there
To meet the child you were, covered with dirt.

It will not hurt you, it simply shows
That you are not alone,
That what you fear is part of you,
That you are both the killer and the kill.

LISA BELLEAR
1961–2006

INTRODUCTION AND EXTRACT CHOICE BY
JAMIE GRANT, POET AND EDITOR

LISA BELLEAR WAS BORN IN MELBOURNE IN 1961. HER SINGLE mother died in Lismore, New South Wales, only weeks after her birth, so she was adopted as an orphan by a family in country Victoria. She was educated at Sacred Heart College, Ballarat, and at Melbourne University, where she was an outstanding student. At the age of twenty she learned for the first time that she was the niece of Australia's first Indigenous-born judge, Bob Bellear. She worked as an academic and a social commentator, and was a prominent activist, radio broadcaster, dramatist, comedian and photographer as well as being a poet. Her poetry, collected in the book *Dreaming in Urban Areas*, is raw, direct and energetic.

DREAMING IN URBAN AREAS
LISA BELLEAR
UNIVERSITY OF QUEENSLAND PRESS, ST LUCIA, 1996, P. 6

Women's Liberation

Talk to me about the feminist movement,
the gubba middle class
hetero sexual revolution
way back in the seventies
when men wore tweed jackets with

leather elbows, and the women, well
I don't remember or maybe I just don't care
or can't relate.

DOROTHY PORTER

1954–2008

INTRODUCTION AND EXTRACT CHOICE BY
DAVID McCOOEY, POET, CRITIC AND ACADEMIC

DOROTHY PORTER WAS BORN IN SYDNEY BUT WAS A MELBOURNE local since 1993. She is best known for her verse novels, beginning with *Akhenaten* (1992). Her second, a lesbian detective novel in verse entitled *The Monkey's Mask* (1994), was a surprise bestseller that was made into a feature film in 1999. As Rose Lucas writes in the *Dictionary of Literary Biography*, Porter 'can be seen as a feminist poet, concerned with the representation and exploration of female experience, female voices, and female—especially lesbian—sexuality'. Porter also wrote young adult fiction, libretti for two operas by Jonathan Mills, and lyrics for a jazz song cycle by Paul Grabowsky.

THE BEE HUT

DOROTHY PORTER

BLACK INC., MELBOURNE, 2009

Lucky

for Andy

There's a damp melancholy
in T'ang poetry
that smudges
the lovely jade
precision.

I love Walt Whitman's
spunky company
but under his bardic
whistling
I can hear his lonely heart
howling
at the turned back
of some deaf rough trade.

So many poets
starve
in the cold faery spaces
between their frost-bitten ears.

How lucky I am
to hear you, darling,
coming up the stairs
to smell the coffee
floating ahead of you
like my favourite incense.

MELBOURNE TAKES THE STAGE

FOR MUCH OF THE NINETEENTH CENTURY MELBOURNE theatre was home to popular or imported entertainment. Victorian stages were dominated by melodramas, pantomimes and farces, and local entrepreneurs such as George Coppin and Bland Holt were more interested in bringing 'stars' from overseas than in fostering home-grown talent.

It was not until early in the twentieth century that a drive for Australian drama was born. From 1909 to 1912 journalist, dramatist and art historian William Moore held annual drama nights in Melbourne showcasing one-act plays. In the 1920s, Louis Esson and the Pioneer Players staged a number of locally written plays, and the company has been credited with accelerating the development of new Australian drama.

Yet these initial movements did not find broad support and it was not until the end of the Second World War that a native dramatic tradition began to truly take hold. This coicided with the growing professionalisation of the amateur repertory companies—the 'little theatre' movement—and the beginning of the subsidisation of the performing arts.

In 1955 the play that would change Australian drama forever was produced—Ray Lawler's *Summer of the Seventeenth Doll*. Touring in Australia and to London and New York, *The Doll* proved the validity and viability of a drama with Australian characters, idiom and themes. It was not until the late 1960s, however, that a broader, alternative theatre tradition began to prosper—a so-called 'new wave' of Australian drama.

The Victorian playwrights of the 1970s have been central to the consolidation of an Australian dramatic tradition. These playwrights

unselfconsciously considered all aspects of Australian society, commonly offering a satirical and political view.

The 1980s saw the success and demise of different types of theatre companies: from the flourishing heights of the Melbourne Theatre Company, to the decline and death of the Australian Performing Group. In addition there was a rise of regional companies, community theatres and cosmopolitan, inner-city venues.

As well as writing for the mainstream companies, contemporary Victorian playwrights are surrounded by numerous outlets for their work in a range of small, semi-professional and (often under-funded) fringe theatres. Contemporary playwrights have continued to dissolve the once-held distinction between high and low culture, and the subject matter of their craft has taken on an international concern as social, technological and touring developments have broadened their sphere of influence.

LOUIS ESSON
1878-1943

INTRODUCTION AND EXTRACT BY GEOFFREY MILNE, HISTORIAN AND CRITIC

SCOTTISH-BORN, AUSTRALIAN-RAISED PLAYWRIGHT AND journalist Louis Esson had eleven of his many plays published. Influenced by Ireland's leading playwrights, Esson sought to pioneer a distinctive Australian folk drama reflecting his own rather idealised brand of socialism. Many of his short and full-length plays are set in the bush, while others celebrate working-class life in town. One of his best remembered plays, *The Time is Not Yet Ripe* (1912), is a city play portraying conservative Prime Minister Sir Joseph Quiverton and his family and circle (especially his daughter Doris) and members of the Socialist Party (notably its oddly aristocratic candidate Sydney Barrett, with whom Doris is in love) on the eve of a national election.

THE TIME IS NOT YET RIPE
LOUIS ESSON
CURRENCY PRESS, STRAWBERRY HILLS, 2008, PP. 6-9

from ACT ONE

Enter SYDNEY BARRETT *as* DORIS *shows* JOHN K. HILL *into the card room, and returns.* BARRETT *advances.*

DORIS: O, Syd! What nice rough cloth! It suits you very well.

BARRET: I am a man of the people.

DORIS: How did you get in?

BARRETT: By what you call the tradesmen's entrance. But Doris—

DORIS: Why are you so absurdly bashful? You are making yourself positively ridiculous ... I told Father.

BARRETT: Was he pleased?

DORIS: Pleased? He went off.

BARRETT: I am glad of that. He so seldom does.

> *He goes to kiss her.*

DORIS: Wait till I shut the door! I can give you only a few minutes alone.

> *She shuts card room door, and returns.* BARRETT *embraces her.*

[*With her head on his shoulder*] O, Sydney, this is all I want. No more. [*Pushing him away*] Sit down. Now! [*Taking a seat*] Do you admire me immensely?

BARRETT: I do. You are quite perfect. But Doris—

DORIS: But what?

BARRETT: You are still wearing jewellery.

DORIS: One can express oneself in jewellery.

BARRETT: Did I not tell you to discard those pearls?

DORIS: Three times.

BARRETT: Have you never thought of the Ceylon diver who held his breath, and went all naked to the hungry shark?

DORIS: Does he mind? You said once you would feel transcendently happy if I permitted you to die for me.

BARRETT: So I would, in a romantic mood. But, Doris, it is time we had a definite understanding. You must give up your jewellery and bridge and Salons and other forms of fashionable frivolity.

DORIS: Does Socialism mean that?

BARRETT: Of course it does.

DORIS: I am not a Socialist, then. I don't believe in it.

BARRETT: You are pursuing an illusory existence. It must end.

DORIS: I wish, Syd, you wouldn't try to reform me. It will be much better for us both if I reform you.

BARRETT: Listen, Doris, you must do as I tell you.

DORIS: You are getting as bad as Father.

BARRETT: What an atmosphere! Bridge and bad politics!

DORIS: Sydney!

BARRETT: Here am I after a four-years' absence, returned to my native land, full of a fine enthusiasm, to find the country stagnant, decadent—and the young Australian, with his bright, fresh mind, untrammelled by the traditions of the past—that is the current phrase—repeating all the popular superstitions, from beer to bishops, of his fog-bound ancestors. Australia is an outer suburb of Brixton. That explains its amazing school of architecture. That explains everything. We are unoriginal, therefore uninteresting.

DORIS: That's all so abstract, isn't it?

BARRETT: We prate of progress, and what is Australia's chief contribution to civilisation? Frozen mutton and the losing hazard. Can you wonder that I am dissatisfied?

DORIS: You always are. You're an idealist.

RAY LAWLER
1921–

INTRODUCTION AND EXTRACT CHOICE BY JULIAN MEYRICK, ACADEMIC

AN ACTOR AND DIRECTOR AS WELL AS A PLAYWRIGHT, RAY Lawler joined the Union Repertory Theatre (later Melbourne Theatre) Company in 1954 and had great success at home and abroad with *Summer of the Seventeenth Doll* the following year. The renowned UK critic Kenneth Tynan praised the play for its 'respect for ordinary people' saying 'we have found ourselves a playwright and we should rejoice'. It is generally regarded as the first indisputably great Australian play. During the 1960s, while resident overseas, Lawler wrote for television and theatre including the dramas *The Piccadilly Bushman* (1961) and *The Man Who Shot the Albatross* (1971). On his return to Australia in the 1970s he added two prequels to *The Doll*—*Other Times* (1976) and *Kid Stakes* (1978)—which taken together form *The Doll Trilogy*. From 1975 to 1987, Lawler was a director and literary manager for the MTC. The studio in the company's new Southbank theatre is named after him.

THE DOLL TRILOGY

RAY LAWLER

CURRENCY PRESS, WOOLLAHRA, 1978, PP. 238–41

Summer of the Seventeenth Doll
from ACT ONE, SCENE TWO

[... BARNEY *mooches over to the French window, standing looking out.*
PEARL, *a little bewildered, appears in the archway. She hesitates, then
speaks tentatively.*]

PEARL: Barney ...

BARNEY: [*turning*] Oh. G'day, Pearl. Come on in.

PEARL: [*nervously*] Shut the window, will you? I want to talk to you.

BARNEY: A bit shy, eh? [*Closing the window*] Well, I can understand that.
[*He smiles vaguely at her. It must be understood here that* BARNEY'S
*instinct for wooing is mechanically reacting at the beginning of this
scene, his mind is on other things. Later on, however, he becomes genu-
inely interested.*]

PEARL: Olive's asked me—

BARNEY: [*interposing*] Wait a minute, first I got to apologise to yer. Roo
says I kicked up a row outside your door last night.

PEARL: Don't you remember?

BARNEY: Well, this p'bably sounds like a bit of bull, but I don't. Most
likely it was all that beer I put away, then it bein' my first night down
here, and Nancy always havin' had that room other times ...
[*He leaves a delicate pause.*]

PEARL: Ye-es. But it was my name you kept yellin' out.

BARNEY: Was it?

PEARL: Pearlie, you kept sayin', it's me, Pearl.

BARNEY: That's interestin'. Even when I didn't know what I was doin', I could still remember your name. Just shows you what an impression you must have made on me.

PEARL: [*still suspicious*] Umm, I don't think you can judge by that. Anyway, it's not what I've come to see you about. Olive said I ought to ...

BARNEY: [*quickly*] Yeah, she told me too—we're to have a quiet little chat. That the idea? Well, there's no reason why you should stand up for it, is there? Take the weight off your feet.

> [*He places a chair for her. She hesitates for a moment and then sits gingerly. He has robbed her of the advantage of a firm opening, and she now starts a little uncertainly.*]

PEARL: It's no business of mine, you understand, and you might reckon I've got a bit of cheek, but there's something Olive didn't tell me when she first asked me if I'd like to be ... [*choosing the word carefully*] a friend of yours.

BARNEY: Kept something back, did she?

PEARL: Yes. [*Girding herself*] Like I say, it's really no business of mine, but until last Saturday I didn't know you had any ... de facto wives.

BARNEY: But I haven't! Ooh, what you mean is my kids? [*As she nods stiffly*] I tipped it'd be like that. Yes, kids I got all right. In three States.

PEARL: [*swallowing hard*] Well, that's it. I didn't want to have to talk to you about it, but Olive said I couldn't walk out without tellin' you, so ...

> [*She makes a move as if to rise, he checks her.*]

BARNEY: Hold on a bit ... did she tell you the rest of it? That I paid maintenance on every one of them till they got old enough to work—that

I'm still payin' for the youngest girl?

PEARL: [*bursting in*] Maintenance? Do you reckon that's the only claim they've got on you? Honest, when I think what their mothers must have gone through! I'm a mother myself, I can … [*Words fail her.*]

BARNEY: You're real mad at me, aren't yer?

PEARL: Yes, I am. There's no excuse for that sort of thing, you're just a no-hoper. You must be!

BARNEY: [*sincerely*] Maybe I am. But I can't help it. Honest. Ever since I was a kid, whenever I've met a good-looking woman, I've always felt like an excited eel in a fish basket.

PEARL: Don't make jokes about it.

BARNEY: I'm not. I know it's nothin' to be proud of—but I'm not gunna apologise for it, either.

PEARL: [*outraged*] And that's that! Just sayin' you're weak gives you the right to run around and have kids wherever you want to—

BARNEY: No, it doesn't. But the ordinary bloke's got a way out, he can get married. There's always been a sorta reason why I never could …

PEARL: [*incredulously*] With children in three States? I'd like to hear of any reason that big!

BARNEY: [*bluntly*] Righto then, you listen. My eldest boys, the two of 'em, are both about the same age.

PEARL: Well?

BARNEY: Well, use your nut, don't you see what it means? Their mothers was in trouble at the same time. Oh, I'm to blame for that, and I'm not saying I ain't, but I was only a silly kid when it happened. Eighteen, I was.

PEARL: Old enough to face up to your responsibilities.

BARNEY: Maybe it is, but it's hardly enough to face up to a big decision like—which of the two was I s'posed to marry? You just think of it: two good decent girls, and you can only make it right for one of them. I nearly went mad. Whichever one of them I married, I thought it'd be a rotten insult to the other. And it would have been. Both of them said so.

PEARL: [*dogged*] You could have done something.

BARNEY: What?

[*She is stumped for an answer.*]

Anyway, I didn't have time. My old man found out about it, and he kicked me out. Gave me a quid and a blanket, nearly twelve o'clock at night. Little place called Makarandi it was, up in New South. Well, that settled it. I knew I 'ad to make some money fast, so I went where the big money was, then—off to Queensland.

PEARL: What you mean is, you run out on the girls!

BARNEY: I was doin' the best I could for everyone. I put me age up to twenty-one, and I worked like a Trojan. Paid all their bills right through, I did, everythin' for both of them. And after that I started payin' maintenance. But I left it up to them which one I was to marry. You decide, I said. [*With long-remembered relish*] Well—they're sitting up there in that little one-horse town in New South Weles still arguin' about it! And I'm as far off marriage as ever I was—'coz if there's one thing I do believe in, it's what Nancy used to say: first come, first served.

DAVID WILLIAMSON
1942–

THE EARLY 1970S WERE BOOM TIMES FOR INDEPENDENT theatre companies and they provided the springboard for David Williamson's career. In 1970 Williamson's first full-length play, *The Coming of Stork*, was produced and in the following year *Don's Party* premiered with the Australian Performing Group at the same time as *The Removalists* was playing at La Mama. With the success of these two plays Williamson was able to give up his job lecturing to concentrate on his writing, and since this time Williamson has become Australia's best-known playwright. Williamson has also written a number of award-winning screenplays and adaptations for film, including *The Year of Living Dangerously*, *Gallipoli* and *Don's Party*.

DON'S PARTY
DAVID WILLIAMSON
CURRENCY PRESS, SYDNEY, 1997, PP. 1–3

ACT ONE

8.40 p.m. Guests are expected any minute. DON *is in the kitchen. He plugs in the television set and begins to adjust it. The audience can't see the screen but can hear the soundtrack.* KATH *is tidying the living room.*

KATH: [*edgy, preoccupied*] Put the peanuts and crisps around, will you?
DON: I'm tuning in the television.
KATH: People will be arriving any minute.

DON: I'm tuning in the television.

KATH: Just switch it on and leave it.

DON: I'm adjusting the vertical hold.

KATH: [*barely controlled*] Just switch it on and leave it.

DON: The picture's rolling.

KATH: Well, it wasn't last night.

DON: Well, it is now.

KATH: Adjust the vertical hold.

DON: That's what I'm doing.

KATH: Could you come back to it? The guests'll be arriving any minute now.

DON: So what!

KATH: They might like something to eat!

DON: I'm adjusting the contrast.

[DON *turns up the sound on the TV. We hear this announcement:*]

TV: Polling closed tonight at eight o'clock and the counting of votes for the 1969 Federal Election has begun. We are now in the Central Tally Room in Canberra and as soon as the results come to hand we will bring them to you. Our panel of experts is standing by ready to interpret voting trends for you, and will be conducting interviews with party representatives throughout the evening. Stay tuned to this channel for a complete coverage of the 1969 Federal Election.

[KATH *glares at him, puts down whatever she's doing, picks up the trays of chips and Twisties, and starts distributing them herself in the living room, banging the trays down unnecessarily hard to give vent to her annoyance.* DON *stands back from the television set, satisfied that it's working.*]

DON: There's no need for you to do it.

KATH: I've done it.

DON: I would've done it.

KATH: [*sharply*] Try and act like a host tonight, will you?

DON: [*complaining*] Cut it out.

　　　[DON *turns down the sound.*]

KATH: It wouldn't take much effort.

DON: Since when have I been rude to guests?

KATH: You usually point them in the direction of the fridge and that's it.

DON: That's all my friends need.

KATH: I can't see the point of coming to a party with the sole intention of drinking yourself into a stupor.

DON: That's not the intention.

KATH: Hmm.

DON: There's a bloody important event on the television tonight. Or perhaps you haven't heard.

KATH: It's just an excuse for a booze-up.

DON: [*flaring*] A booze-up? That's why I've been out there all day handing out how-to-vote cards? Just an excuse for a booze-up?

KATH: I've never noticed Cooley showing much interest in politics.

DON: [*indignant*] Cooley's left of centre!

KATH: The only thing Cooley's left are a trail of used up women and more empty beer bottles than any one else in Australia.

　　　[*Pause.*]

　　Who's he bringing tonight?

DON: [*surly*] I don't know.

KATH: Is he bringing that air hostess?

David Williamson's

DON'S PARTY

THE PLAY THAT CHANGED A GENERATION

DON: No.

KATH: What happened to her? She was nice.

DON: I don't know.

KATH: Probably got too serious.

DON: Probably.

KATH: Who's he bringing, then?

DON: I told you. I don't know. He just flew down from Sydney yesterday.

KATH: Could you tell him to leave his gymnastics until he gets back to the motel? He woke Richard last time.

DON: He didn't wake him. The air hostess did.

KATH: It's frightening for a young child.

DON: It was probably frightening for the air hostess. Would you like a drink?

KATH: I can't. I'm on tablets.

DON: They were supposed to make you happy. Bloody shithouse tablets.

KATH: [*sharply*] Lay off. And try and show me a little bit of affection tonight, will you?

DON: I show you a lot of affection. You just don't notice it.

KATH: Neither does anyone else.

     [*Pause.*]

If you want the honest truth, I think that your friends are the biggest bunch of pricks I've ever met.

DON: Yeah … well, it would be a pretty sparse party if we threw one for your friends. Unless we invited the pottery class.

KATH: Why did you marry me if I'm so bloody mundane?

DON: I didn't want my personality swamped.

JACK HIBBERD
1940–

INTRODUCTION AND EXTRACT CHOICE BY
GEOFFREY MILNE, HISTORIAN AND CRITIC

JACK HIBBERD WAS A LEADING FIGURE IN THE 'NEW WAVE' of Australian playwriting in Melbourne in the late 1960s and early 1970s. He had numerous plays produced at La Mama and the Pram Factory, one of his biggest successes being the country wedding play *Dimboola*, which has been frequently revived. His work is marked by great verbal dexterity, with puns deriving from medicine, the classics and modern literature and music. He especially embraced monodrama, the most remarkable example being *A Stretch of the Imagination* (1972), featuring the octogenarian misanthropist Monk O'Neill and his bitter-sweet memories of real or imagined past glories.

A STRETCH OF THE IMAGINATION
JACK HIBBERD
CURRENCY PRESS, SYDNEY, 1973, PP. 8–10

It's several years since I had a visitor. You could hardly classify him as a visitor … it was unpremeditated. He had lost his way. Stacked his Harley Davidson. Lost his way. Took a wrong turning. Don't we all? He staggered in here lacquered with dust and dung, his plimsolls in shreds, as desiccated as an old parsnip. Make yourself at home, I said. Pull up a chair. There was only one. Would you fancy a bite to eat, a beaker of

something cool, a hot poultice, a kick in the crotch? Good. Relax, pal,
while I repair to the Coolgardie and knock up a snack. How'd you go
a Mayfair ham? You could do with a spot of salt. Bendigo pig. My lips
smack in anticipation … my last tin … usually open one at Christmas
… exhume a few fine memories …

> (He enters the hut.
>
> MONK is heard inside, whistling and at work.
>
> He shouts from inside.)

I meant, consume. Sorry. Born and bred in the district. They cultivate
a good tomato up that way. Shits on Adelaide.

> (He appears with a lump of ham in aspic on a plate, a screw-top
> lemonade bottle filled with weak black tea, and a champagne glass.
>
> He sets them down on the table.)

There we are, son.

> (He takes a fork from a pocket of his shorts and places it beside the
> plate. He takes a pen-knife from the other pocket, opens it, and
> puts it on the other side of the plate.
>
> He pours tea into the glass.)

Into it.

> (Pause.)

Perhaps you'd welcome a tomato? No? A radish? Odourless onion?
Broad beans? Caustic soda?

> (Pause.)

All home grown.

> (Pause.)

You'd prefer a stick of celery? You would. What? Yes, you heard cor-
rectly. It's not a celery district. Too hot. Too dry. Too wet. Cactus yes,

celery no. The sirocco, you know. Flattens the pricks.

(Pause. He stands and watches.)

Difficult bastard.

(Pause.)

It's not often I have the privilege of a guest.

(Pause.)

Excuse the lack of etiquette, but what's your name? Mort? Mort Lazarus. (To himself) A four-by-two. I never knew there was gold around One Tree Hill. (To MORT) I'm Monk. Monk O'Neill. Delighted to make your acquaintance. (Shaking hands) Welcome to the oasis.

(Pause.)

What brought you to One Tree Hill? The view? Magnificent is it not? (Gazing afar) A panorama of dust, anthills, and dead grass. Naught else. Except for the occasional bull turd.

(Pause.)

How is it? Great. Mind if I join you?

(MONK takes the lump of meat and chews into it.)

(After a while) Finished?

(He pockets the fork and pen-knife, takes the plate, and goes into the hut, still eating.

Pause.

A clatter is heard as MONK trips over inside, and swears.

Pause.

MONK appears in the doorway, wearing an old tennis shade. He picks his teeth with the corkscrew on his pen-knife.)

It's just on dusk, Mort. Little point in setting off now, replenished as you are. Stay the night. Join me in a round of canasta, euchre, Russian roulette, you prick. Sorry. I didn't mean that. Listen, stretch out under the stars. Sleep is what you need, son. I'll fetch you a blanket. You'll be as warm as a woman.

I did just that ... brought out a thick old Onkaparinga ... and laid it gently over his slumbrous limbs ...

(Pause.)

Don't mention it, chief.

(Pause.)

Asleep already.

(MONK tip-toes to the hut and enters.

Pause.

He puts his head out the door and whispers.)

See you in the morning, Mort. Bright and early ... for your departure.

(He disappears.

Long pause.

MONK comes out, slowly, wearing a large hat.)

I walked out next morning and found him still asleep. Dead. A corpse. There'd been a snap frost during the night. The quicksilver was most reluctant to rise that morning. Killed off all my fucking tomatoes, too. There he was. Stiff and cold. I removed the blanket and dragged him into the sun. Thought he might thaw out, stage a recovery. He didn't. I returned, after a doomed attempt to revive the tomatoes, to find him swarming with bull-ants, maggots and parakeets. Quite a banquet. I tossed a few handfuls of quicklime over his remains, remembered a sad prayer or two, and lowered him into the pit of no return. Just there where the clock sits at night. No suspicious circumstances.

(Pause.

MONK walks across to the table, picks up the clock and reads the time.)

No.

(He puts the hat over it.

BARRY DICKINS

1949 –

INTRODUCTION AND EXTRACT CHOICE BY
GEOFFREY MILNE, HISTORIAN AND CRITIC

BARRY DICKINS IS ONE OF OUR QUIRKIEST PLAYWRIGHTS AND one of our most prolific. He is also one of our funniest, and his style is anything but orthodox; with very rare exceptions, he does not write 'well-made plays'. However, he invariably approaches his subjects—often battlers and underdogs, and sometimes 'real' people—with deep compassion lurking below a surface of bad puns, verbal dexterity and a free-wheeling dramatic structure. He has often turned to monodrama, as in this excerpt from his 1982 *Lennie Lower*, a celebration of the life of the noted Sydney newspaper columnist of the 1930s.

LENNIE LOWER

BARRY DICKINS

JEFFREY FIDDES (GENERAL EDITOR), YACKANDANDAH PLAYSCRIPTS,
MONTMORENCY, 1982, PP. 31–3

Gretel Packer, the famous yatch's wife was more than keen on me to do an
interview with Noel Coward when he came to Sydney. What a joke.

Weppy give me a dink to the Victoria Hotel. How left wing.

I seen Coward standing there. He looked embalmed. Like a trout in a tux-
edo. No joking or nothing, you could just about do up your tie in his hair
it was that shiny. And his mo! You got a headache looking at it.

Weppy and me are blotto. Turped. Drunk as owls.

"Go on Lower, aren't you game?"

says Weppy, all of five foot nothin'.

"Don't like poms,"

I said, sulking behind me moose pate and stringbag fulla runners.

We were into the fitness at the time.

"Bulldust, you're just scared of Noel Coward,"

he says. And fronts him.

Weppy leaning against Coward's fly. Well, he uses my standard intro;

"Mr. Coward, sulking over there behind the moose pate lurks none
other a personage than LENNIE W. LOWER, Australia's foremost
humorist."

Silence. Coward is like ice. Weppy looked like he was gonna go to sleep.
All them pommy snobs snickering at him. Like he was a real mug or
something.

And Wep's no mug. Greatest black and white press artist in Australia.

So I rushed over there. Never needed the crutches at the time. And I grabbed Coward by the throat and I said,

[*As if throttling invisible Noel Coward*]

"What's wrong with you? You fuckin' great big pommy poofta."

[*Pause*]

Frank Packer sacked me a hundred and eleven times for that.

[*Begins cross to customer side. Stops.*]

Oh, I'd been sacked before. But he was in earnest this time.

[*Completes cross to customer side stool. Sits. Starts typing. Stops.*
Upstage cross. Indicates typewriter.]

See this ordinary article? See this innocent calculator of jokes?

This thirty-five bob tickler of ribs? I hate it. I hate it because it breathes life into the dailies and takes the life outa me.

[*Looking up to Frank*]

Listen Frank, I tell you what let's do. How'd you go writing the jokes, pal? Let me sit in the office smoking the cigars.

I mean, come on Frank, it's either one or the other. Well, what do you reckon? Could you do it?

[*Looks back. Glances at typewriter. Grabs whisky*]

I tried to knock meself up a feed last night.

Had to go up the back and get a claw-hammer and a box of inch nails to keep it still. I'm all right slamming in a few nails.

[*Skaals drink*]

Not so good at … I don't know how to live.

[*Look up to Dad*]

Dad … Dad … What would you do in my boots tonight? You'd know what to do. I don't know anyone. Is that funny?

Is that a laugh? Is that a decent joke? Everybody reads me, Dad, and

they all laugh like billy-o and I'm lonely.
I speak to the steam floating out of a packet of fish and chips.
When I rip the paper apart I see Frank Packer.
   [*Looks at glass in hand*]
I'm that drunk lately I don't remember if I just had that last drink.

HANNIE RAYSON
1957–

INTRODUCTION AND EXTRACT CHOICE BY JULIAN MEYRICK, ACADEMIC

WITH A BACKGROUND IN COMMUNITY THEATRE (SHE WAS A co-founder of Theatreworks in 1980), Rayson has worked for every major theatre company in Melbourne, and most interstate. Her plays include *Please Return to Sender* (1980); *Mary* (1981); *Room to Move* (1985), which won an AWGIE Award for Best Original Stage Play; *Hotel Sorrento* (1990) — later made into a film — another AWGIE-award winner, also attracting the NSW Premier's Literary Award; *Life After George* (2000), which won the 2001 Helpmann Award for Best New Australian Work; *Inheritance* (2003), another Helpmann Award winner; and *The Glass Soldier* (2007). She has also written for the television dramas *Seachange* and *Seven Deadly Sins*. Hailed by critic Kate Herbert 'the jewel in the crown of Melbourne theatre', her plays often focus on ethical decisions, especially in the early plays with largely female casts, but lately with a broader social focus.

INHERITANCE

HANNIE RAYSON

CURRENCY PRESS, SYDNEY, 2003, P. 13–16

SCENE TEN

GIRLIE *and* MAUREEN *walk down the main street of Rushton.* GIRLIE *is on her frame,* MAUREEN *assisting.*

GIRLIE: You'll never guess what she's done now.

MAUREEN: Who?

GIRLIE: Dibs. She's gone and asked the wogs.

MAUREEN: The Pappases? From the pub? Christ.

GIRLIE: Honest to God. [*To the audience*] I said to Maureen—this is my daughter-in-law, Maureen.

MAUREEN: [*to the audience*] G'day.

GIRLIE: [*to the audience*] I said to Maureen, she's asking people willy-nilly and it's not as if she'll get more food in. We're looking after the grog—our side—but I don't know what she thinks we're all gonna eat. My sister is a very Christian woman—Dibs—but when it comes down to it—she's as mean as all get-out. It's the Presbyterian in her. Stingy. Here, cross the road. I don't like walking past the pub.

MAUREEN: They know it was you dobbed them in, you know.

GIRLIE: Serves them right. [*Yelling*] Pack o' cheats!

MAUREEN: Sshh.

GIRLIE: You can't water down your vodka and expect to get away with it.

MAUREEN: If it's true.

GIRLIE: It's true. Fifteen dollars for a plate of steak and chips. Daylight robbery. There's people in this town can't afford a raffle ticket.

MAUREEN: People gotta eat.

GIRLIE: When we ran the place—never charged anything over a tenna. [*Yelling*] They're thieves, those Greeks!

MAUREEN: Girlie!

GIRLIE: Blow-ins. And they don't pay tax neither. Who do they think pays for the roads and the schools and that?

MAUREEN: Their boy put in a good game in the ruck last Saturday.

GIRLIE: Still a wog.

MAUREEN: I hear young Felix has got himself a new girlfriend. [*Pause.*] Japanese.

GIRLIE: Oh, Christ All-Bloody-Mighty.

MAUREEN: I thought he was a homo.

GIRLIE: I dunno why the mother doesn't put her foot down.

MAUREEN: Julia?! She probably put him up to it. She's a big shot in the whole multicultural racket. That's her job down there.

GIRLIE: What about I order a couple dozen sausage rolls?

MAUREEN: Yeah. Maybe some party pies.

GIRLIE: Some quiche lorraines, too, I reckon.

MAUREEN: Are they the ones with bacon in them?

GIRLIE: So what?

MAUREEN: We need something for the vegetarians.

GIRLIE: Bugger the vegetarians.

JOANNA MURRAY-SMITH

1962–

INTRODUCTION AND EXTRACT CHOICE BY
GEOFFREY MILNE, HISTORIAN AND CRITIC

JOANNA MURRAY-SMITH HAS HAD PLAYS PRODUCED SINCE the late 1980s, but her career bloomed after 1990 with a string of plays for Melbourne's Playbox Theatre Company and more recently the Melbourne Theatre Company. Her always finely crafted, small-cast studies of middle-class people in crisis feature clipped, circular, repetitive dialogue, complex characters and meticulously plotted revelations. Mostly identified as a Melbourne phenomenon, she has enjoyed frequent overseas success. Her 'breakthrough' 1985 play *Honour*—winner of the Victorian Premier's Literary Award in 1986 —focuses on middle-aged couple Gus and Honor, their daughter Sophie and a young writer Claudia, for whom Gus falls.

HONOUR

JOANNA MURRAY-SMITH

CURRENCY PRESS, SYDNEY, IN ASSOCIATION WITH PLAYBOX THEATRE
CENTRE, MONASH UNIVERSITY, MELBOURNE, 1995, PP. 23–6

HONOR: Your father's left.
    [*Pause.*]
    What I mean to say is. Ah. Your father has left me.
SOPHIE: What?

HONOR: He's not. It seems. It seems he's not in love with me anymore.

SOPHIE: What?

HONOR: He's – ah – found someone else.

SOPHIE: He's found someone else?

HONOR: Yes.

SOPHIE: He's left you for someone else?

HONOR: Yes.

SOPHIE: Dad's left you for another woman?

HONOR: Yes.

     [Long silence.]

SOPHIE: Who?

HONOR: Claudia.

SOPHIE: Claudia?

HONOR: Yes.

SOPHIE: Who's doing the profile for that book?

HONOR: Yes.

     [Silence.]

SOPHIE: Isn't she? Isn't she?

     [Pause.]

She's my age.

HONOR: She's twenty-nine.

     [Silence.]

SOPHIE: That fucking bastard.

HONOR: Yes.

     [Silence.]

SOPHIE: He actually said that. That he was leaving?

HONOR: Yes.

SOPHIE: You're telling me he just came home and said he wanted out?

HONOR: That's what happened.

SOPHIE: When?

HONOR: Tuesday.

[*Silence.*]

SOPHIE: Well, were there signs?

HONOR: I don't know –

SOPHIE: There must have been – there must have been signs –

HONOR: I didn't see them –

SOPHIE: You must have – have blocked them –

HONOR: I saw no signs –

SOPHIE: You must have blocked them. There are *always* signs –

HONOR: I don't know. Does it matter?

SOPHIE: You have to be alert. You have to be so alert. You have to notice everything –

HONOR: We've been married thirty-two years –

SOPHIE: Because people don't realise the little codes they use to speak to each other –

HONOR: I don't care –

SOPHIE: You don't care –

HONOR: I don't care about codes –

[*Pause.*]

SOPHIE: How, then? How – Can you – I don't get it. On Tuesday, he – ?

HONOR: Tuesday. Night. He. He told me. He broke down. He isn't himself. Or is he? Is he himself?

SOPHIE: Well, is it unusual? Have I been completely stupid? Is this Dad? I mean is this what he does?

HONOR: No.

SOPHIE: No?

HONOR: Not what he does. I think.

SOPHIE: He said he's leaving you?

HONOR: I think this is a – I think this is a – a once off kind of – I think he met her and –

SOPHIE: Well that's very important, isn't it?

HONOR: Is it?

SOPHIE: Isn't it? Is he in love with her or – or out of – out of love – you know, out of love with you?

[*Too painful to answer. Silence.*]

Oh Mum –

HONOR: No. No! It'll kill me if you do that. It'll kill me.

[*Silence.*]

She came here for dinner. I cooked her a very nice watercress soup and stuffed veal. Stuffed veal. I think we had. We had homemade florentines with coffee. I thought, young single woman and all that. Could probably do with a good meal. She had it.

SOPHIE: It's his crisis. It's his fucking belated mid-life crisis – It's his. What? What's he proving? That he can still fuck! Is that it?! That he can fuck girls! Why doesn't he get a fucking psychiatrist instead!

HONOR: He didn't mean to hurt you –

SOPHIE: I'm not hurt!

HONOR: You should talk to him. Maybe you're just seeing things from my view – If you talk to him –

SOPHIE: What?

HONOR: He didn't want – He doesn't know what he's doing –

SOPHIE: You're defending him!

HONOR: Well –

SOPHIE: [*incredulous*] You're defending him?

HONOR: He can't help it! He can't help it!

SOPHIE: What?

HONOR: He's in love with her for Christ's sake.

SOPHIE: You're *explaining* him to me?

HONOR: He can't force himself to do the right thing –

SOPHIE: Yes he can! Yes he can! Lots do!

HONOR: He can't make himself love me!

SOPHIE: And all this. All this – this here. You. All of it. Me. That. All the time. All of us. That's what? That's what? That's shit? That's nothing?

HONOR: I don't know.

SOPHIE: Jesus, Mum. [*Beat.*] You have to fight!

HONOR: Fight what?

SOPHIE: *Him*. Fight him.

HONOR: Why?

SOPHIE: You can't. You're just. Why are you like this?

HONOR: Like what?

SOPHIE: You're just *accepting* it –

HONOR: What choice do I have –

SOPHIE: You should be angry – You should – You should – You're just –

HONOR: What?

SOPHIE: It's so typical –

HONOR: What's typical?

SOPHIE: To be the – The – Martyr. To be the martyr. To just accept this as if – as if it's inevitable. As if it's deserved –

HONOR: [*exasperated*] That's not fair! What can I do? You want me to cut all the arms off his jumpers? Or burn down this house? What good is it?

SOPHIE: That's so – that's so passive! That's so passive. That's – that's such a – You're such a product of your generation –

HONOR: Does that make it easier for you? To see me that way?

SOPHIE: You've got to – You've got to take control of your life –

HONOR: What life?

SOPHIE: Where's he living? Where's he living? With her?

HONOR: I don't know.

SOPHIE: Well, what going on? Is it temporary or what? Have you talked to him?

HONOR: Not – well, just that I'll stay here in the house for the moment. And we'll talk "when we've both calmed down" in quotation marks.

SOPHIE: I'm going to talk to him.

HONOR: I just want – I'm not defending him, but – you should remember. He's always going to be your father. He can stop being my husband. Or her – lover. But he'll never not be your father. So don't –

SOPHIE: What?

HONOR: Don't –

SOPHIE: What?

HONOR: Don't *become* me, alright?

MEAN STREETS AND BACK ALLEYS

V ICTORIAN CRIME WRITING CAN CLAIM SOME QUITE illustrious beginnings. Within thirty years of the colony's birth, local crime writers were establishing the genre's place in the popular mind, both here and overseas.

Ellen Davitt's *Force and Fraud* is considered Australia's first mystery novel and was originally serialised in the *Australian Journal* in 1865—only five years after the world's first full-length mystery novels were published elsewhere. Another woman who made her mark was Mary Fortune, one of the world's first writers of detective fiction. But perhaps the best-known of nineteenth-century crime novels was *Mystery of a Hansom Cab*, the world's first crime bestseller.

After the Second World War a number of Victorian writers made a serious impact, both here and overseas. June Wright contributed six crime novels—many with a female protagonist—and Sidney Courtier published twenty-six novels. Overshadowing these writers—by weight of numbers alone—was William Henry Williams: writing as Marc Brody he published an incredible sixty-one 'pulp' novels in only five years. But it wasn't until crime writing's 're-birth' in the 1980s that a strong Australian identity pervaded all aspects of the genre.

Victorian-born Peter Corris was the first of this new wave of crime writers, and Victorian writers have excelled in selling their works both here and overseas. Peter Temple was the 2007 recipient of the world's most renowned award for crime writing—the Gold Dagger—and Garry Disher has twice received the German Crime Fiction Award. Others such as Shane Maloney and Kerry Greenwood have also excelled: Greenwood has published thirty-eight novels, including sixteen in the Phryne Fisher series, while Maloney's Murray Whelan novels have been published in the UK, Germany, France, Britain, Japan, Finland and the US.

MARC BRODY

2/-

SINNER— OR LATER

FERGUS HUME

1859-1932

INTRODUCTION AND EXTRACT CHOICE BY DERHAM GROVES, ACADEMIC

FERGUS HUME WAS BORN IN POWICK, ENGLAND, EDUCATED in Otago, New Zealand, and worked in Melbourne, Australia. He was a solicitor. His first novel, *The Mystery of a Hansom Cab*, was set in goldrush-era Melbourne and written in the style of Emile Gaboriau. When local publishers showed no interest in the story, Hume published 5000 copies of it himself in 1886 (one year before *A Study In Scarlet*, the first Sherlock Holmes novel by Arthur Conan Doyle). The first edition sold out in three weeks and was reprinted many times over, although early on Hume sold the rights for £50. In 1888 he returned to England to write full-time. The success of *The Mystery of a Hansom Cab* was due in no small measure to the novelty of its local settings. In the following exerpt Mr Calton, 'one of the leading lawyers of the city', is given a tour of Little Bourke Street in Melbourne by Mr Kilsip, a detective.

THE MYSTERY OF A HANSOM CAB

FERGUS HUME

SELF-PUBLISHED, PRINTED BY KEMP & BOYCE, MELBOURNE, 1886, PP. 102-3

THE BRILLIANTLY LIT STREET, WITH THE NEVER-CEASING STREAM of people pouring along; the shrill cries of the street Arabs, the rattle of vehicles, and the fitful strains of music, all made up a scene which fascinated him, and he could have gone on wandering all night, watching the myriad phases of human character constantly passing before his eyes. But his guide, with whom familiarity with the proletarians had, in a great measure, bred indifference, hurried him away to Little Bourke-street, where the narrowness of the street, with the high buildings on each side, the dim light of the sparsely scattered gas lamps, and the few ragged looking figures slouching along, formed a strong contrast to the brilliant and crowded scene they had just left. Turning off Little Bourke-street, the detective led the way down a dark lane, which felt like a furnace, owing to the heat of the night; but, on looking up, Calton caught a glimpse of the blue sky far above, glittering with stars, which gave him quite a sensation of coolness.

"Keep close to me," whispered Kilsip, touching the barrister on the arm; "We may meet some nasty customers about here."

Mr. Calton, however, did not need such a warning, for the neighbourhood through which they were passing was so like that of the Seven Dials in London, that he kept as closely to the side of his guide, as did Dante to that of Virgil in the Infernal Regions. It was not quite dark, for the atmosphere had that luminous kind of haze so observable in Australian twilights, and this weird light was just sufficient to make the darkness visible. Kilsip and the barrister kept for safety in the middle of the alley,

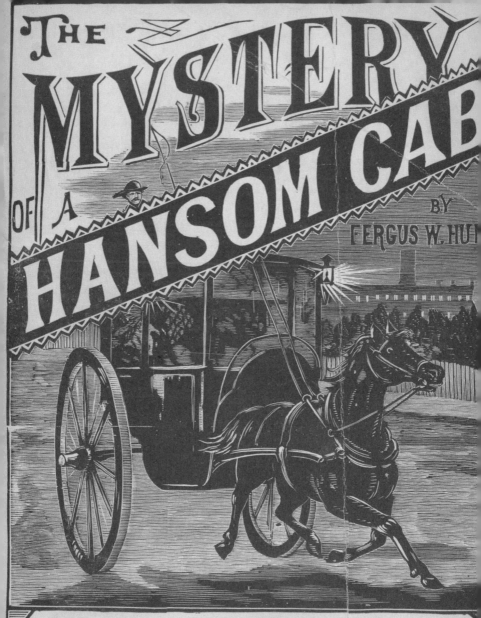

THE MYSTERY
OF A HANSOM CAB

BY
FERGUS W. HUME

New York:
J. S. OGILVIE PUBLISHING COMPANY,
57 ROSE STREET.

so that no one could spring upon them unaware, and they could see some-
times on the one side, a man cowering back into the black shadow, or on
the other, a woman with disordered hair and bare bosom, leaning out of
a window trying to get a breath of fresh air. There were also some chil-
dren playing in the dried-up gutter, and their shrill young voices came
echoing strangely through the gloom, mingling with a bacchanalian sort
of song a man was singing, as he slouched along unsteadily over the rough
stones. Now and then a mild looking string of Chinamen stole along, clad
in their dull hued blue blouses, either chattering shrilly, like a lot of par-
rots, or moving silently down the alley with a stolid Oriental apathy on
their yellow faces. Here and there came a stream of warm light through
an open door, and within, the Mongolians were gathered round the gam-
bling tables, playing fan-tan, or leaving the seductions of their favourite
pastime, and, gliding soft-footed to the many cook-shops, where enticing-
looking fowls and turkeys already cooked, were awaiting purchasers.
Kilsip turning to the left, led the barrister down another and still nar-
rower lane, the darkness and gloom of which made the lawyer shudder, as
he wondered how human beings could live in them.

"It is like walking in the valley of the shadow of death," he muttered
to himself, as they brushed past a woman who was crouching down in a
dark corner, and who looked up at them with an evil scowl on her white
face. And, indeed, it was not unlike the description in Bunyan's famous
allegory, what with the semi-darkness, the wild lights and shadows, and
the vague undefinable forms of men and women flitting to and fro in
the dusky twilight.

At last to Calton's relief, for he felt somewhat bewildered by the
darkness and narrowness of the lanes through which he had been taken,

the detective stopped before a door, which he opened, and stepping inside, beckoned to the barrister to follow. Calton did so, and found himself in a low, dark, ill-smelling passage, at the end of which they saw a faint light. Kilsip caught his companion by the arm and guided him carefully along the passage. There was much need of this caution, for Calton could feel that the rotten boards were full of holes, into which one or the other of his feet kept slipping from time to time, while he could hear the rats squeaking and scampering away on all sides. Just as they got to the end of this tunnel, for it could be called nothing else, the light suddenly went out, and they were left in complete darkness.

JUNE WRIGHT

1919–

INTRODUCTION AND EXTRACT CHOICE BY DERHAM GROVES, ACADEMIC

JUNE WRIGHT published six crime novels between 1948 and 1966. All six were set in or around Melbourne. *Murder in the Telephone Exchange* (1948), her first, and *Faculty of Murder* (1961), her fifth, are perhaps her best. Wright's highly original nun-detective, Mother Mary St Paul of the Cross (Mother Paul for short), appears in the last three novels. Interesting local settings, feisty female protagonists and credible social situations characterise Wright's work. These skills are showcased in the following exerpt from *Murder in the Telephone Exchange*. Maggie Byrnes, a spirited young telephonist, who functions as the novel's detective-narrator, describes her landlord Mrs Bates.

MURDER IN THE TELEPHONE EXCHANGE

MURDER IN THE TELEPHONE EXCHANGE

JUNE WRIGHT

HUTCHINSON & CO., MELBOURNE, c. 1948, PP. 44–5

WHEN I FIRST SET EYES ON MY LANDLADY I HAD THE IMPRESSION she was too unreal to exist. She was more a product of the imagination; the type of character Dickens would have created and revelled in. She was fairly tall, clad always from head to bunion-swollen feet in respectable black, with a surprisingly enormous bosom pushed high to her chin by old-fashioned corsets. Her face was long and narrow, and there was something wrong with her tear-ducts. She was compelled to wipe her pale blue eyes continually. It gave her the appearance of a mastiff dog, which was rather apt. According to the saga of her life, which she had told me in serial form over a space of months, she had had a dog's life. This canine career included a drunkard of a husband, who, having deserted her many years previously, turned up frequently demanding money. I often heard Mrs. Bates haranguing him when I was hanging stockings over my window-sill to dry. Her Billingsgate, or perhaps I should say Fitzroy language, to make it more local, must have been totally at variance with the weird religious creed to which she was always trying to convert me.

In addition to the affliction of her eyes, she had had an operation for goitre, which had in some way impaired her windpipe. This caused her to wheeze every few words she spoke. It held Clark fascinated the first time he met her. She carefully inspected all the men whom her young ladies, as she called us, brought to the house, and later issued gloomy warnings as to the general infidelity and unsteadiness of the male sex. Clark had had a bad start. He was too good-looking to be trusted at all, though I had seen Mrs. Bates relax a little under his infectious smile.

KERRY GREENWOOD
1954–

INTRODUCTION AND EXTRACT CHOICE BY SUE TURNBULL, ACADEMIC

IN 1989, BARRISTER KERRY GREENWOOD INTRODUCED THE character of wealthy heiress and private detective Phryne Fisher onto the Melbourne scene of 1928. Inspired partly by Leslie Charteris's character of *The Saint*, Phryne embodied a feminist re-imagining of the hard-boiled dick as a glamorous aesthete with a passion for food, good sex and justice. The narrative voice is ebullient and witty. Much delight is to be had in the descriptions of people and place. The Windsor Hotel is a great favourite of Phryne's, as is Madame Olga's in Collins Street where Phryne goes shopping with her newly acquired lady's maid, Dorothy. First and foremost, however, Phryne is a woman of action who always puts things to rights and always gets her man—or woman.

COCAINE BLUES
KERRY GREENWOOD
ALLEN & UNWIN, CROWS NEST, 2005, PP. 8–9

PHRYNE LEANED ON THE SHIP'S RAIL, LISTENING TO THE SEAGULLS announcing that land was near, and watched for the first hint of sunrise. She had put on her lounging robe, of a dramatic oriental pattern of green and gold, an outfit not to be sprung suddenly on invalids or those of nervous tendencies – and she was rather glad that there was no one on deck to be astonished. It was five o'clock in the morning.

There was a faint gleam on the horizon; Phryne was waiting for the green flash, which she had never seen. She fumbled in her pocket for cigarettes, her holder, and a match. She lit the gasper and dropped the match over the side. The brief flare had unsighted her; she blinked, and ran a hand over her short black cap of hair.

'I wonder what I want to do?' Phryne asked of herself. 'It has all been quite interesting up until now, but I can't dance and game my life away. I suppose I could try for the air race record in the new Avro – or join Miss May Cunliffe in the road-trials of the new Lagonda – or learn Abyssinian – or take to gin – or breed horses – I don't know, it all seems very flat.'

'Well, I shall try being a perfect Lady Detective in Melbourne – that ought to be difficult enough – and perhaps something will suggest itself. If not, I can still catch the ski season. It may prove amusing, after all.'

At that moment there came a fast, unrepeatable grass-green flash before the gold and rose of sunrise coloured the sky. Phryne blew the sun a kiss, and returned to her cabin.

SHANE MALONEY
1953–

INTRODUCTION AND EXTRACT CHOICE BY SUE TURNBULL, ACADEMIC

MAN OF MANY PARTS, SHANE MALONEY PRODUCED THE FIRST instalment in the ongoing adventures of Labor Party apparachik Murray Whelan in 1994. More densely written than some of the subsequent books in the series, *Stiff* contained all the hallmarks of Maloney's stock in trade: wry descriptions of the Melbourne social landscape in the 1980s, witty deflations of political pomposity, and comic set pieces involving Murray in awkward and often hilarious predicaments. Recently separated from his politically ambitious wife Wendy and living with his young son Red in the northern suburbs in the midst of comic mayhem and occasionally murder, the hapless Murray succeeds almost despite himself in solving crime and achieving a successful political career.

THE MURRAY WHELAN TRILOGY
STIFF
SHANE MALONEY

TEXT PUBLISHING, MELBOURNE, 2004, PP. 3–4

IT ALL STARTED ON ONE OF THOSE MISERABLE WET MONDAY mornings when, come nine o'clock, half of Melbourne is still strung out bumper-to-bumper along the South-eastern Freeway. I had just dropped my son Red at school, and as I swung my clapped-out old Renault into Sydney Road the thought of all those Volvo and Camira drivers stewing away behind their windscreen wipers brought a quiet smile to my lips. Not that I bore them any personal animosity, you understand. It was just that if God wanted to punish the eastern suburbs for voting Liberal, She wouldn't hear me complaining.

I could afford to feel like that because the Brunton Avenue log-jam was miles away. Where I lived, north of town, the toiling masses tended to start their toiling a little earlier in the day, and most of those that still had jobs were already at work. By nine the rush hour had already come and gone. Apart from a few hundred light industrial vehicles and the occasional tram disgorging early shoppers, women in head-scarfs mainly, I had the northbound lane to myself.

Not that I was busting a gut to get to work. No clock was waiting for me to punch it, and I couldn't see the pile of paper on my desk bursting into flames if left undisturbed a little longer. The fifteen minutes it took me to drive to work provided one of my few moments of solitude all day and I liked to make the most of it. As I drove I read the paper.

This was less dangerous than it sounds. I'd already studied the broadsheets over breakfast, and the *Sun* was the kind of tabloid easily absorbed while doing something else—shelling peas, for instance, or operating a lathe. I had it spread open on the passenger seat beside me, and whenever I hit a red light or got stuck behind a slow-moving tram I skimmed a couple of pages. The spring racing carnival had just begun, so the emphasis was on horseflesh, fashion and catering. Just A Dash was favourite, black was big, and interesting things were being done with asparagus. Agreement was unanimous—four years in and the eighties were holding form as the most exciting decade ever.

PETER TEMPLE
1946–

INTRODUCTION AND EXTRACT CHOICE BY SUE TURNBULL, ACADEMIC

BORN IN SOUTH AFRICA, JOURNALIST PETER TEMPLE MOVED to Australia in 1980. His first crime novel, *Bad Debts*, was published in 1996 to critical acclaim and in 2007 his eighth book, *The Broken Shore* (2005), won a swag of awards including the prestigious Duncan Lawrie Dagger from the British Crime Writers' Association. *The Broken Shore* introduces the character of Detective Joe Cashin, who has returned to his home beat after being severely injured in the line of duty in Melbourne. As with all Temple's crime novels, the Australian landscape is brought into sharp focus as we first meet Cashin walking his dogs. In spare but vivid prose, Temple offers perceptive social commentary about the changing nature of rural life. Dialogue, especially between men, is laconic, the resonance residing less in the words than in the gestures that accompany them.

THE BROKEN SHORE

PETER TEMPLE

TEXT PUBLISHING, MELBOURNE, 2006, PP. 1–2

CASHIN WALKED AROUND THE HILL, INTO THE WIND FROM THE SEA. It was cold, late autumn, last glowing leaves clinging to the liquidambars and maples his great-grandfather's brother had planted, their surrender close. He loved this time, the morning stillness, loved it more than spring.

The dogs were tiring now but still hunting the ground, noses down, taking more time to sniff, less hopeful. Then one picked up a scent and, new life in their legs, they loped in file for the trees, vanished.

When he was near the house, the dogs, black as liquorice, came out of the trees, stopped, heads up, looked around as if seeing the land for the first time. Explorers. They turned their gaze on him for a while, started down the slope.

He walked the last stretch as briskly as he could and, as he put his hand out to the gate, they reached him. Their curly black heads tried to nudge him aside, insisting on entering first, strong back legs pushing. He unlatched the gate, they pushed it open enough to slip in, nose to tail, trotted down the path to the shed door. Both wanted to be first again, stood with tails up, furry scimitars, noses touching at the door jamb.

Inside, the big poodles led him to the kitchen. They had water bowls there and they stuck their noses into them and drank in a noisy way. Cashin prepared their meal: two slices each from the cannon-barrel dog sausage made by the butcher in Kenmare, three handfuls each of dry dog food. He got the dogs' attention, took the bowls outside, placed them a metre apart.

The dogs came out. He told them to sit. Stomachs full of water, they did so slowly and with disdain, appeared to be arthritic. Given permission to eat, they looked at the food without interest, looked at each other, at him. Why have we been brought here to see this inedible stuff?

Cashin went inside. In his hip pocket, the mobile rang.

GARRY DISHER

1949–

INTRODUCTION AND EXTRACT CHOICE BY SUE TURNBULL, ACADEMIC

ALREADY RECOGNISED AS A LITERARY NOVELIST, SHORT STORY writer and successful children's author, Garry Disher produced the first of his Wyatt crime series in 1991. Inspired by the 'caper' crime novels of 'Donald E Westlake writing as Richard Stark', Disher's Wyatt is a thief who finds crime addictive. He is a hard man, not easy to like, but a character the reader comes to respect as he operates according to his own strict moral code. Wyatt is a professional and good at his job, always avoiding unnecessary violence. But the world he inhabits is uniformly bleak, from the closely observed inner life of a city to the beautifully described flat grey landscape around Hastings. The Wyatt novels are always elegiac in tone.

KICKBACK

GARRY DISHER

ALLEN & UNWIN, NORTH SYDNEY, 1991, PP. 65–6

BEFORE GOING FOR THE GUNS ON TUESDAY MORNING, WYATT checked out of the Gatehouse. He never spent more than one night in a place when he was setting up a job. He checked into a cheap hotel nearby, put his remaining cash in a money belt around his waist, and entered the Underground at Parliament Station. He caught a train that went through Burnley. Out of habit he sat at the end of the carriage, where he had a clear view of the aisle and the entry and connecting doors. He kept his hand on the knife in his pocket. That was habit, too. But knives were useful. People respected the swift threat of a blade where a gun or a raised fist simply flustered them.

The carriage was almost empty. Two men, one elderly, the other about forty, sat near the middle doors. Three middle-aged women were going home with their shopping. Wyatt listened to them comparing the hairdressing salons in Myer and David Jones. Two young Vietnamese men, quick and glittering, sat at the far end of the carriage. Across from Wyatt was an overweight teenage mother wearing stretch jeans and scuffed moccasins. She had trouble keeping still, and shouted rather than spoke endearments to a squawling child in a pusher. There was graffiti on the windows, the script bold and mocking.

He got off at Burnley Station and stood at the timetable board watching others get off, watching for lingerers. He saw the young mother light a cigarette and shake the pusher. She joined a huddle of people at the exit gate, people who could easily be her parents, siblings, neighbours. They disappeared into the flat, exhausted streets. Sour poverty and contention and mindless pride, Wyatt thought. He'd grown up in a suburb like this. Everyone had talked solidarity, but he'd never seen it.

Other trains came in and pulled out again. He left the station and walked to Cowper Road, a narrow street of sodden workers' cottages and grimy workshops. Cars heaved across small craters in the road surface, throwing up gouts of oily water.

Number twenty-nine was a corrugated-iron shed about thirty metres deep. A sign above the door said Burnley Metal Fabricators. On a smaller sign was the word 'office' and an arrow that pointed left to a turn-of-the-century cottage which shared a wall with the shed.

Apart from the patchy lawn and a chained Alsatian on the verandah, there was no sign of life at the cottage. The curtains were imitation lace. Steel bars secured the windows. Keeping a wary eye on the Alsatian, Wyatt mounted the steps to the door. The dog opened and closed an eye and yawned squeakily. Its tail flapped. Wyatt pressed the buzzer.

D URING THE NINETEENTH CENTURY MOST BOOKS for younger readers were driven by the moral concerns of their authors. The desire to push adult concerns onto children has since faded in children's literature. The market has now grown to include teenage readers, and writers speak more directly to young people.

The tone of many early children's books published in Victoria was authoritative and mirrored the political and cultural mores of the day. Works that seem racist and didactic by today's standards were commonplace, and cultural allegiances to Britain were proudly displayed.

From the 1940s, the morality and ideological aspirations of authors became less evident; the stories took over and the tone and subject matter began to shift. Until the 1950s and 1960s the gender roles of characters had remained steadfastly conservative, with boys taking part in adventure stories while girls remained mostly indoors. This meant that most female characters were afforded a greater inner life than male characters, but this was to change.

A new respect for young readers emerged in the second half of the twentieth century. Writers, illustrators, editors and publishers began creating bold, imaginative, sophisticated books in a variety of genres. Innovative local publishers have been vital in promoting the works of local authors and illustrators and in exporting their works to the world, in English and in translation.

There is now greater diversity of subject matter, approach and style in children's literature, with storylines and characters reflecting the lives of young people, rather than the idealised imaginings of adults.

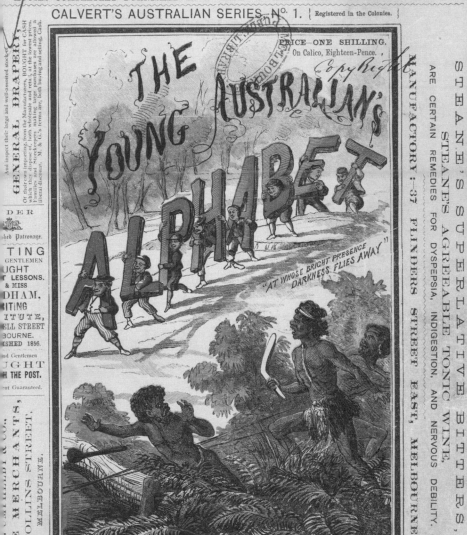

CALVERT'S AUSTRALIAN SERIES. Nº 1. | Registered in the Colonies.

PRICE—ONE SHILLING.
On Calico, Eighteen-Pence.

Copyright

THE YOUNG AUSTRALIAN'S ALPHABET

"AT WHOSE BRIGHT PRESENCE DARKNESS FLIES AWAY"

J. CALVERT.

A for **AUSTRALIA**
    Which I am told,
Is famous for Corn,
For Wool and for Gold.

B is the **BLACK-FELLOW**
    We can all see,
Lazily sleeping
Under a tree.

C is a **COCKATOO**
    With a gay crest,
He chatters and thinks he is
One of the best.

D for the **DIGGERS**
    Who busily seek,
For Gold and for Jewels
Down by the creek.

YOUNG AUSTRALIAN'S ALPHABET

To THIS DAY ALPHABET BOOKS ARE VERY POPULAR WITH both adults and children alike. Given the simplicity of form, with each letter corresponding to recognisable items from daily life, alphabet books readily show the preoccupations of the era in which they were written. This book—*The Young Australian's Alphabet* (1871)—is beautifully illustrated and coloured, but its representation of Indigenous Australians is quite disturbing to many contemporary readers.

EDWARD WILLIAM COLE
1832–1918

EDWARD WILLIAM COLE ARRIVED IN MELBOURNE IN 1852 drawn, like thousands of others, by the lure of gold. After a disappointing stint as a prospector, Cole's natural entrepreneurial talents led him to various jobs including purveyor of lemon cordial, property developer, photographer, labourer, pie-seller and finally bookseller. He started by selling books out of a wheelbarrow but eventually built a book emporium that would run the length of a city block—Cole's Book Arcade. As well as having a flair for business, Cole was an idealist and a devoted family man. In 1879 he published the first edition of *Cole's Funny Picture Book*, which was a compilation of puzzles, poems, stories and pictures cut out from newspapers and other publications of the time, mixed with his own original drawings and essays. It was an immediate hit and went on to sell a million copies, as well as winning the hearts of many generations of Australian children.

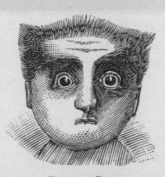

Do not Stare.

IDA RENTOUL OUTHWAITE
AND
ANNIE RATTRAY RENTOUL
1888–1960 (OUTHWAITE), 1882–1978 (RENTOUL)

IDA RENTOUL OUTHWAITE WAS A MAJOR FIGURE IN CHILDREN'S
book illustration during the early twentieth century, enjoying
regular exhibitions in Paris, London and Australia in the 1920s
and 1930s. From her school days Ida worked with her sister, the
writer Annie R Rentoul, and they enjoyed their first major success
in 1903 when six illustrated stories were published in *New Idea*.
Outhwaite is perhaps best known for *Elves and Fairies*, a luxuri-
ous book published in 1916. Her sister Annie wrote the verses for
Elves and Fairies and Outhwaite's husband, Grenbry Outhwaite,
edited the book.

ELVES AND FAIRIES OF IDA RENTOUL OUTHWAITE

IDA RENTOUL OUTHWAITE

VERSES BY ANNIE R RENTOUL, EDITED BY GRENBRY OUTHWAITE

LOTHIAN BOOKS, MELBOURNE, 1916, PP. 3-4

Moonrise.

Moonrise comes,
  Pushing through the ti-tree;
Moonrise comes,
  With her wand of pearl;
Moonrise comes,
  I can hear the Fairies;
Softer than a wattle-bud
  Their wings uncurl.
Hush, hush, hush!
  I can hear the Fairies;
Softer than a wattle-bud
  Their wings uncurl.

Lamplight comes,
  Looking through the windows;
Lamplight comes,
  With her torch of gold;
Lamplight comes,
  I can hear the children;

Softer than a flannel flower
  Their eyelids fold.
Hush, hush, hush!
  I can hear the children;
Softer than a flannel flower
  Their eyelids fold.

Dreamland comes,
  Closing in the wide world;
Dreamland comes,
  Fairy tales are true;
Dreamland comes,
  I can hear the children
Dancing with the Fairies
  On the moss and dew.
Hush, hush, hush!
  Don't you wake the children
Dancing with the Fairies
  On the moss and dew.

MARY GRANT BRUCE

1878-1958

MARY GRANT BRUCE WAS ONE OF AUSTRALIA'S MOST SUCCESSFUL
children's authors of the early twentieth century. Born in Sale,
Bruce worked as a journalist for both *The Age* and the *Leader*
before turning her hand to novels for children. She is best known
for her Billabong series, published between 1910 and 1942. The
first of these—*A Little Bush Maid* (1910)—found publication
in serial form in the *Leader*. These adventure stories set in the
bush were immensely popular, exhorting positive bush values
and shaping the way many Australians thought about the land.
Although Bruce's attitudes about race and class are now frowned
upon, her novels were significant for featuring female protago-
nists who were both strong and capable.

A LITTLE BUSH MAID

MARY GRANT BRUCE

WARD, LOCK & CO., MELBOURNE, 1910, PP. 12–14

NORAH HAD NEVER KNOWN HER MOTHER. SHE WAS ONLY A
tiny baby when that gay little mother died—a sudden, terrible blow, that
changed her father in a night from a young man to an old one. It was
nearly eleven years ago now, but no one ever dared to speak to David
Linton of his wife. Sometimes Norah used to ask Jim about mother—
for Jim was fifteen, and could remember just a little; but his memories
were so vague and misty that his information was unsatisfactory. And,

after all, Norah did not trouble much. She had always been so happy that she could not imagine that to have had a mother would have made any particular difference to her happiness. You see, she did not know.

She had grown just as the bush wild flowers grow—hardy, unchecked, almost untended; for, though old nurse had always been there, her nurseling had gone her own way from the time she could toddle. She was everybody's pet and plaything; the only being who had power to make her stern, silent father smile—almost the only one who ever saw the softer side of his character. He was fond and proud of Jim—glad that the boy was growing up straight and strong and manly, able to make his way in the world. But Norah was his heart's desire.

Of course she was spoilt—if spoiling consists in rarely checking an impulse. All her life Norah had done pretty well whatever she wanted—which meant that she had lived out of doors, followed in Jim's footsteps wherever practicable (and in a good many ways most people would have thought distinctly impracticable), and spent about two-thirds of her waking time on horseback. But the spoiling was not of a very harmful kind. Her chosen pursuits brought her under the unspoken discipline of the work of the station, wherein ordinary instinct taught her to do as others did, and conform to their ways. She had all the dread of being thought   silly" that marks the girl who imitates boyish ways. Jim's rare growl, "Have a little sense!" went farther home than a whole volume of admonitions of a more ordinarily genuine feminine type.

She had no little girl friends, for none was nearer than the nearest township—Cunjee, seventeen miles away. Moreover, little girls bored Norah frightfully. They seemed a species quite distinct from herself. They prattled of dolls; they loved to skip, to dress up and "play ladies";

and when Norah spoke of the superior joys of cutting out cattle or coursing hares over the Long Plain, they stared at her with blank lack of understanding. With boys she got on much better. Jim and she were tremendous chums, and she had moped sadly when he went to Melbourne to school. Holidays then became the shining events of the year, and the boys whom Jim brought home with him, at first prone to look down on the small girl with lofty condescension, generally ended by voting her "no end of a jolly kid," and according her the respect due to a person who could teach them more of bush life than they had dreamed of.

IVAN SOUTHALL
1921–2008

INTRODUCTION AND EXTRACT CHOICE BY BERNADETTE WELCH, ACADEMIC

UNDOUBTEDLY ONE OF THE MOST INFLUENTIAL AUSTRALIAN writers for young people, Ivan Southall published prolifically from 1933 to the late 1990s. He was well known both in Australia and overseas for his stories of survival, where young people, separated from adults, deal with threatening floods, bush fires, road accidents or plane crashes. Use of an interior monologue style and more complex characters and responses characterised his later work and provoked critical acclaim and some controversy. His most important works were published in the 1960s and 1970s when he won four Children's Book Council of Australia Book of the Year Awards and the British Carnegie Medal.

JOSH

IVAN SOUTHALL

ANGUS & ROBERTSON, SYDNEY, 1971, PP. 146-7

SO IT ENDS IN ANGER AND DISGRACE AND DISTRESS AND everything else you'd care to put your tongue around. You name it, Josh, and it ends that way. You're the daddy of all the Plowmans, that's what they tell you, and maybe they're right. You've ripped through Ryan Creek like a runaway truck. Every kid in town hates your guts.

Every kid outside in the street. Every kid waiting at the cricket ground. Every kid asking himself what sort of a louse is Josh.

Everyone up there at the gate; Aunt Clara apologizing, apologizing, apologizing to everyone in sight.

No one told me the match was so important. I thought it was a kid's game. Grown-up umpires. People coming to watch. I couldn't have played anyway. It's out of my class. What's wrong with Aunt Clara? Push, push, push. I didn't tell her I was a champion. I only told her I played. Wasn't that good enough?

Home to Mum. That's next. She'll ask what's the trouble – you're not expected back till Saturday or Sunday or maybe Monday?

The trouble, Mum, they tell me, is that I'm a louse. But I'm a fair enough kid, aren't I? I don't go stirring up trouble. I don't hate people. The neighbours don't lock up their houses when they see me coming. I haven't an enemy in the world that I can think of right now. But from the minute I hit the place everything went wrong.

They had it in for me like I was poison; even Aunt Clara turned nasty when things wouldn't go the way she wanted. And that I'll never understand. She took their side, not mine, and they were wrong all along the line. They never even tried to be right.

Josh you didn't behave like a Plowman, did you?

I behaved like me.

You must be a Plowman, Josh. You must wear it all over you not knowing it's there. A Plowman doesn't need to be wrong. He can be objectionable when he's right.

Mum, should I have played? Should I go even now? All these kids waiting for their game. Kids coming from Croxley, miles and miles. Betsy hating me. But you don't know about her. There's something about Betsy that strikes a little bell. I'd go if she asked me; I reckon I'd run all the way. You can't always put a principle first, can you, Mum? Sometimes you've got to compromise. It looks that way if Aunt Clara's any guide. She's turning herself inside-out so often I don't know which face is properly hers. Honest, Mum, it's a laugh. Everyone threatening they'd get me if I went to the match, then holding me up to ransom when I decided not to play.

If I wasn't a Plowman none of this would have happened to me. If stupid Bill hadn't brought those pants it wouldn't have happened. If Laura hadn't jumped from the bridge, if Rex hadn't tripped me, if Aunt Clara hadn't taken my book of poems, if I hadn't come away from you and Dad, if a hundred things hadn't happened it wouldn't have happened at all. I ask you. It's a horrible rolling wheel. What hope has a fellow got? The day he gets born it starts turning and he can't even jump out of the way. What's wrong with people? Have they always got to find a mug they can blame?

ALAN MARSHALL
1902–1984

EXTRACT CHOICE BY HELEN CHAMBERLIN, CHILDREN'S BOOK PUBLISHER

Alan Marshall is perhaps best known for the first volume of his autobiography, *I Can Jump Puddles* (1955). More than three million copies have been sold, and many hundreds of thousands of young readers have been uplifted by Marshall's inspirational battle with polio, and the courage and optimism with which he lived. During his life, Marshall was awarded an OBE (1972), an AM (1981) and a Soviet Order of Friendship (1977); he continues to be honoured by the annual Alan Marshall Short Story Competition.

I CAN JUMP PUDDLES
ALAN MARSHALL
PUFFIN BOOKS/PENGUIN BOOKS, CAMBERWELL, 2004, PP. 7–10

NOT LONG AFTER I BECAME PARALYSED THE MUSCLES IN MY legs began to shrink, and my back, once straight and strong, now curved to one side. The sinews behind my knees tightened into cords that tugged at my legs till they gradually bent and became locked in a kneeling position.

The painful tension of the twin sinews behind each knee and the conviction that if my legs were not soon straightened they would always remain in their locked position, worried my mother who kept calling on Dr Crawford to prescribe some treatment that would enable me to move them normally again.

Dr Crawford, uncertain of how Infantile Paralysis developed, had watched my mother's attempts to bring life back into my legs by massaging them with brandy and olive oil – a cure recommended by the school teacher's wife, who claimed that it cured her rheumatism – with a slight frown of disapproval, but, after remarking 'It can't do any harm', left the question of my immovable legs till he had made further enquiries about the complications being experienced by victims in Melbourne.

Dr Crawford lived at Balunga, the township four miles from our home, and would only visit patients in outlying districts when the case was an urgent one. He drove a jogging grey horse in an Abbot buggy with the hood half raised, so that the lining of scalloped blue felt, acting as a background, presented him to the best advantage as he bowed and flourished his buggy whip to those who passed. The Abbot buggy established him as the equal of a squatter, but not the equal of a squatter who had an Abbot buggy with rubber tyres.

He was a man with a readily available knowledge of the simpler diseases.

'I can say confidently, Mrs Marshall, that your son has not got the measles.'

But Poliomyelitis was a disease of which he knew very little. He had called in two other doctors for consultation when I first became ill, and it was one of these who announced that I had Infantile Paralysis.

Mother was impressed by this doctor, who seemed to know so much, and turned to him for further information, but all he would say was, 'If he were a son of mine I would be very, very worried.'

'I'm sure you would,' said my mother dryly, and never had any faith in him from then on. She believed in Dr Crawford who, when the other

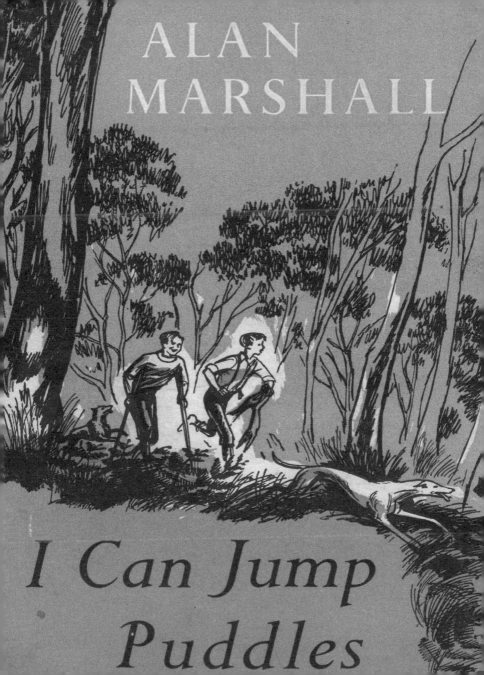

ALAN
MARSHALL

*I Can Jump
Puddles*

two doctors had gone, said, 'Mrs Marshall, no one can tell whether your son will be crippled or not, or whether he will live or die. I believe he will live, but it is in God's hands.'

This pronouncement comforted my mother but my father reacted in quite a different way. It brought from him the observation that Dr Crawford had now admitted he knew nothing about Infantile Paralysis.

'Once they tell you you're in God's hands you know you're done,' he said.

The problem of my contracting legs was one that Dr Crawford eventually had to face. Troubled and uncertain, he beat his pudgy fingers in a soft tattoo upon the marble top of the washstand beside my bed while he looked down on me in silence. Mother stood beside him, tense and still, like a prisoner awaiting sentence.

'Well, now, Mrs Marshall, about these legs … M-m-m-m, yes … I'm afraid there is only one thing we can do. He's a brave boy. That's fortunate. We just have to straighten those legs. The only way is to force them down. They must be forced straight. The question is: how? The best way, I think, would be to lay him on the table each morning then press your weight upon his knees till they straighten. The legs must be pressed flat on the table. Say, three times. Yes, three times would be enough, I think. Say, two on the first day.'

'Will it be very painful?' my mother asked.

'I'm afraid so.' Dr Crawford paused, then added, 'You will need all your courage.'

Each morning when my mother laid me on my back on the kitchen table, I looked at the picture of the frightened horses that hung upon the chimney above the mantelpiece. It was an engraving of a black horse and a white horse crowding together in terror while a jagged streak of lightning projected out of the dark background of storm and rain and hung poised a few feet in front of their distended nostrils. A companion picture on the opposite wall showed them galloping madly away, their legs extended in rocking-horse fashion and their manes flying.

Father, who took all pictures seriously, sometimes stood looking at these horses with one eye half closed to aid his concentration while he assessed their value as hacks.

Once he told me: 'They're Arabs all right, but they're not pure. The mare's got windgalls, too. Look at her fetlocks.'

I resented any criticism of these horses. They were important to me. Each morning I fled with them from jagged pain. Our fears merged and became a single fear that bound us together in a common need.

My mother would place her two hands upon my raised knees then, with eyes tightly closed so that her tears were held back by her clenched lids, she would lean her weight upon my legs forcing them down till they lay flat upon the table. As they straightened to her weight my toes would spread apart then curve down and round like the talons of a bird. When the sinews beneath my knees began to drag and stretch I would scream loudly, my eyes wide open, my gaze on the terrified horses over the mantelpiece. As my toes curved in their agonised clutching, I would cry out to the horses, 'Oh! horses, horses, horses ... Oh! horses, horses ...'

JOHN MARSDEN
1950–

EXTRACT CHOICE BY HELEN CHAMBERLIN, CHILDREN'S BOOK PUBLISHER

JOHN MARSDEN IS ONE OF AUSTRALIA'S BEST LOVED AUTHORS of young adult fiction, providing realistic representations of young people's lives. His first book, *So Much to Tell You* (1987), was written to counter his students' lack of interest in reading. Marsden has enjoyed tremendous success ever since with his trademark gritty and intelligent writing. Marsden's most popular work has been the Tomorrow series; its first title, *Tomorrow, When the War Began*, has been reprinted more than thirty times. Marsden has received numerous prizes, notable mentions and nominations for a number of awards including CBCA Book of the Year and the Lloyd O'Neil Award for Service to the Australian Book Industry.

WINTER
JOHN MARSDEN
PAN MACMILLAN, SYDNEY, 2000, PP. 18–19

I DON'T KNOW HOW LONG I STAYED AWAKE. IT WAS STRANGE. The house, empty of people and furniture and life, felt more alive than any other house I'd been in. More alive than the Robinsons'. More alive than Ralph and Sylvia's. More alive than my Adelaide grandparents'.

I wondered as I lay there if maybe this house would only feel alive to me. Maybe to anyone else it would be more like a museum. A graveyard. Maybe this house came awake for only one person on earth. Maybe it had been waiting for me all this time.

Gradually the feelings got more specific. At first I'd been looking at a painting from a distance. Now I was close to it, seeing the brightly coloured people, the warm petunias in a blue vase, the flames of the fire. I could hear the little sounds people make as they go from room to room. The shush of clothes against a door. The scrape of a foot on the floor. The push of air as someone moves along the corridor. Then the murmur of voices. A cough, a rustle of newspaper, the clink of a coffee cup.

The voices were the most tantalising. I couldn't quite hear what they were saying. I couldn't distinguish a single word. It sounded like adults, the kind of conversation between people who have known each other a long time. A comfortable, easy conversation. A couple of comments, then silence for a while, then a few more sentences. I wanted to get up and join them. But I knew what would happen if I did. Suddenly I knew, with the certainty of memory. A great tingle ran through my body as my mind and my ears played out the scene.

Dad would say, 'Hello, young lady. I thought you were meant to be in bed.'

'I'm thirsty,' I said.

'That's not very original,' Mum said. 'Stay there, Phillip. I'll get it. Now, Winter, one little drink of water and then straight back to bed, OK?'

All those times I'd cried myself to sleep at the Robinsons', it had been a kind of stifled sobbing. I never wanted to be caught. So the tears had seeped out like they were from a tap turned off hard, but still leaking slowly, reluctantly.

Now I cried in a new way. I cried without restraint. I wept like a four-year-old, for the parents I'd lost, for the years I'd been without them, for the parents I'd never see again. My life stretched in front of me, and it looked lonely.

Yet at the same time I knew there was nowhere else on earth I wanted to be. Here at Warriewood was as much comfort as I could hope for. To be in this house, in my own bed, in my own bedroom, to hear those sounds and to feel the live presence of my family from years ago, was like being held close in my mother's arms. That could never happen again in my lifetime, but to have this hint of it, this reminder, seemed to take me back to a time that for twelve years had been beyond the edge of my consciousness, beyond the territory in which I had been living.

ROBIN KLEIN
1936–

INTRODUCTION AND EXTRACT CHOICE BY PAM MACINTYRE, ACADEMIC

BORN IN KEMPSEY, NEW SOUTH WALES, KLEIN SPENT MOST of her writing life in the Dandenongs. Her more than forty books— picture books, novels, short stories and poems—appeal across a wide readership. Characterised by shrewd observation and compassion for the outsider, her writing has an overriding sense of humour. She is known for her skill in creating lovable characters, such as the tiny, vegetarian dinosaur *Thing* (1983, CBCA Junior Book of the Year 1984). Her spirited and individual girls are exemplified by the irrepressible Penny Pollard who features in five novels from 1983 to 1989, and hypochondriac, drama queen Erica Yurken (in *Hating Alison Ashley*, published in 1984 and filmed in 2005). Klein was awarded the Dromkeen Medal in 1991.

HATING ALISON ASHLEY

ROBIN KLEIN

PUFFIN BOOKS/PENGUIN BOOKS, RINGWOOD, 1984, PP. 36–7

I SLAMMED THE KITCHEN DOOR SO HARD THAT THE PLASTIC tulips and plastic maidenhair fern on the hall table fell off. I stomped into my room and Jedda's, which was 90 per cent her room and the rest left over for me. I slammed that door, too, and then sat down and had a good cry in front of the mirror.

I always enjoyed having a good cry. The part of me that wanted to be an actress stood aside and looked on whilst I was bawling. I carefully studied the effect of my hooked hands clawing through my hair, and the best way to blink so that the tears rolled down evenly.

'It's not fair!' I sobbed into my hands. 'Life is full of injustice!' Then I thought of another good line, trying it out with different facial expressions. 'Just one more mile for to tote the weary load,' I said, and it sounded beautiful, though very sad and depressing. I cried some more, and wound it all up with a very powerful statement that always sounds exactly right when you want to end a crying session.

'I wish I were dead!' I said. I said it five times, each time stressing a different word and listening to the result, and then dried my eyes and felt a bit better. I looked round for something I could do to pay Jedda back for having to share a room with her. And for keeping me awake at night making hoof noises in her sleep. She made them with the length of her tongue clamped up against her palate. (I investigated one night with a torch.)

She had about a thousand little plastic model horses all over her 90 per cent of the room, even on top of the wardrobe. I went around and laid each one on its back, so they looked as though they'd been stricken with a serious horse-disease.

Then I got out my magnifying mirror and had a good look at myself in the strong light. I wasn't pretty, but actresses shouldn't be, anyhow. What they really need are dynamic and compelling looks. I felt that I had dynamic and compelling cheekbones, and also a warm, generous mouth. (Though Valjoy said it was just plain big.)

But while I was examining my face in the mirror, I kept thinking of Alison Ashley. Suddenly I craved to look like her, and talk like her and have a mother and a car like hers, and the same clothes and pretty manners, and that she would let me be her best friend. Even if I hated her. I thought gloomily that Alison Ashley most likely never in her life was sent to her room for swearing. Probably she didn't even know any bad words, though going to Barringa East would soon fix that. And if she ever did get sent to her room, she would probably sit down and clean her nails, which never got dirty anyhow, or use the time to revise her tables which she already knew off by heart. Or tidy all her socks into paired rolls. And furthermore, I bet that every six months when she went to the dentist, she never had cavities.

Life was full of injustice.

GRAEME BASE

1958–

GRAEME BASE CAME TO AUSTRALIA FROM ENGLAND AT THE age of eight, attending Melbourne High School and then studying graphic design at Swinburne Institute of Technology. His alphabet book *Animalia* has made him a huge success both here and overseas. It took over three years to produce and has sold over two million copies. As well as being an internationally renowned picture book illustrator, Base is also a musician, which may explain the rhythms of language that sing through his books.

ANIMALIA

GRAEME BASE

VIKING KESTREL, RINGWOOD, 1986

ANDY GRIFFITHS AND TERRY DENTON
1950– (GRIFFITHS), 1961– (DENTON)

ANDY GRIFFITHS AND TERRY DENTON ARE RENOWNED FOR creating a range of humorous books for boys, such as *The Bad Book* (2004). In many ways they carry on the tradition started by Paul Jennings with his publication of *Unreal!* in 1985. Terry Denton has illustrated books for children's authors such as Paul Jennings and Mem Fox, and both Denton and Griffiths have enjoyed great success with their *Just* series of books. Griffiths is also well known for his books *The Day My Bum Went Psycho* and *The Cat on the Mat is Flat*.

THE BAD BOOK
ANDY GRIFFITHS AND TERRY DENTON
PAN MACMILLAN, SYDNEY, 2004, P.2

Bad Humpty Dumpty

Humpty Dumpty spray-painted the wall
He covered it with his offensive scrawl.
All the King's horses and all the King's men
Confiscated his spray-can
    and smashed his head in.

SONYA HARTNETT

1968–

INTRODUCTION AND EXTRACT CHOICE BY AGNES NIEUWENHUIZEN, WRITER

IN 2008 SONYA HARTNETT WAS AWARDED THE ASTRID Lindgren Memorial Award, the world's richest prize for young people's literature. The citation declares: 'Sonya Hartnett (Australia) is one of the major forces for renewal in modern young adult fiction. With psychological depth and a concealed yet palpable anger, she depicts the circumstances of young people without avoiding the darker sides of life. She does so with linguistic virtuosity and a brilliant narrative technique; her works are a source of strength.' Hartnett's work (almost twenty books since her first at age sixteen) is more lauded internationally than at home where her often dark vision together with her fearless dedication to her material and characters resist categorisation in terms of themes or audience. More than any Australian writer she has challenged notions of what young people can, should and will read.

SLEEPING DOGS

SONYA HARTNETT

VIKING/PENGUIN BOOKS, RINGWOOD, 1997, PP. 1–2

THE DOGS DO NOT EVER REALLY SLEEP. SOMETIMES THEY CLOSE their eyes, often for long periods at a time, but always there remain one or two watchful in the dark, and while these are so the pack can be considered to be awake. They lie on their sides and their ribs rise

and fall with the heat, their tongues hang out and collect the dust. They stroll and the chains come after them, making an irregular music. Occasionally they meet in swift and snarling collision, the noise worse than the damage done: they do this simply to relieve the boredom. Their night vision is good and they follow the activities of the night, the travelling of the moon. Nothing alarms them enough to make them bark. Morning brings them to their feet.

At first she thinks the weight is an animal of some kind, wandered into the room and drawn by the sight of her, and it is not for some moments that she realises it is Jordan who has slipped uninvited into bed beside her. She closes an arm around his shoulders and without opening her eyes she knows what he is wearing: overalls and nothing else, he's been up and working early and smells of milk and hay. Though it is morning the day is already hot, she can feel the warmth sunk through his skin, and she knows the caravans will be flaring in the sun, the dam glittering like a diamond, the trees bowed breathless, but that her bedroom is dark and chill, dewy with its own shade. She knows that Jordan is here stealing time, has planned and plotted this moment of quiet between them, and she curls her hand around his, lets his hair tickle her face without becoming cross for it. He lies still for a minute or more, and then sits up on an elbow so he can kiss her and look at her face and touch her closed eyes. He whispers, 'Happy birthday, Michelle.'

And then he is gone, leaving her in the same dreamy state that he'd found her, but awake enough to wonder if any other brother or sister will remember that today she turns twenty-three. Today they are slaughtering a sheep, but not as an act of celebration.

ISOBELLE CARMODY

1958–

EXTRACT CHOICE BY HELEN CHAMBERLIN, CHILDREN'S BOOK PUBLISHER

ISOBELLE CARMODY IS ONE OF AUSTRALIA'S MOST SUCCESSFUL authors of fantasy for young adult readers. Carmody started her first novel, *Obernewtyn*, when she was only fourteen years old, and the *Obernewtyn Chronicles* continue to this day. Since 1996 Carmody has won six Aurealis awards.

THE GATHERING

ISOBELLE CARMODY

PUFFIN BOOKS/PENGUIN BOOKS, RINGWOOD, 1993, PP. XI–XIII

Sometimes you get a feeling about a thing that you can't explain; a premonition of wrongness. Mostly you ignore it the way you would a little kid tugging at your sleeve. You think: what do kids know anyhow?

We drove into the outskirts of Cheshunt at the tail end of a cold crisp day, that was fading to gold. Sunshine slanting through the car window rested in my lap, warm and heavy as a cat.

I was sleepy and a bit woozy from reading my way through a stack of comics. As a rule I am not the kind of guy who goes in for stories about superheroes from Krypton or talking ducks and dogs. I like *National Geographic*, but I was reading these comics because the solicitor had sent them in a box along with a lot of my father's things that had not sold at auction.

My mother thought comics were rubbishy. She only read factual books and medical journals. I had just been a little kid when my parents were divorced, and they had not kept contact but I always had a clear picture of him in my mind as a big serious man. The comics were a surprise and made me wonder what there was about him that I did not know. Naturally I had tried asking my mother but as usual she said she couldn't remember what he used to read, and that it was A Long Time Ago. She drives me crazy the way she acts so secretive about him, especially now.

Suddenly she coughed in the dry fussy way she has of getting my attention before she says something. I waited for her to go on again with her usual speech of us making a new start, but she just nodded sideways.

'That's your new school, Nathanial.'

Your school, I thought, because she chose it, just like she chose all the others. Her face had a closed look and she was staring straight ahead, concentrating on the road.

So I looked.

The school was a square, slab-grey complex set on an asphalt island in the middle of a common, running away to dry, bare-looking flatlands. She had told me Cheshunt was close to the sea. 'You can go to the beach on weekends,' she had said, as if it were across the road from our new house. Except there was no sign of the sea and the skyline bristled with pipes belching smoke into the sky.

Closer to the school, I noticed there were no trees or shrubs around the buildings. In fact, Three North looked a lot like a concentration camp. The few bushes along the roadside were stunted and shrivelled, with empty branches on the side that bore the brunt of the gritty wind flowing across the low hills and over the school. Cold air blew through the window, a bitter blast straight from the arctic.

I lifted my hand to close the window, but it was shut. I looked around but all of the windows were wound up. Even the vents were closed. There was no way that wind could get into the car, yet I could see the fine downy hairs on my arm flatten under its force.

I looked at my mother, who wore only a light, sleeveless shirt. She did not notice the wind, though her hair was whipping into her face and eyes.

Fear crept through skin and bone and folded itself in my chest as I looked back at the school and felt that wind; the same kind of shapeless terror I felt when she took me to look at my father in his coffin before they closed it and put him in the ground.

'You don't have to,' she had said nervously, after doing a song and dance to get me there. It bothered her that I asked her so many questions about him. Her wanting me to see the body was so bizarre that I guessed she had this stupid idea that I would forget about him once I saw that he was really dead and gone. But when it came to it, she seemed jittery and uneasy. Maybe she was a bit scared herself, of what we would see. I went forward, drawn by dread and morbid curiosity.

He had been much thinner than I remembered. It seemed as if death had shrunken him, sucked the bigness out of him. His hair had gone straight and his limbs were stiff as a dried-flower arrangement.

'He's so small,' my mother had said in a shocked whisper, as if he was sick instead of dead; as if loud voices would disturb him.

Looking down at that strange, still face, I had barely been able to control the watery horror in my gut. I was suddenly terrified of being so close to a dead body; terrified that by staying there I might somehow catch death.

That's how I felt, staring out of the car window at Three North; like

I was looking at something wrong and unnatural; something dead; something bad that might be catching. Might get up and come after me.

And the old nightmare seemed to hover about me, almost real, one stage from visible; the nightmare of running through a dark, wild forest with a monster after me. A shambling, leering thing with a shark's smile, whose reeking breath filled the air around me; the monster that was, since the funeral, sometimes my father, and above, a bloody, full moon riding high in the black night.

But I just sat, still as a bone, tongue glued to the roof of my mouth, eyes watering from the force of the wind.

The car glided around the corner and I let the memory of what had happened slip through the fingers of my mind like fine sand.

Because a feeling like that has no more business being in my life than a dead father.

A LITERARY
WALKING TOUR OF MELBOURNE

MELBOURNE PROVIDES A WONDERFUL LIVING landscape, perfect for visiting some of the many landmarks that illustrate our rich literary heritage.

A walking tour of Melbourne's literary history naturally begins with the area's first inhabitants, the Wurundjeri people. **THE KOORIE HERITAGE TRUST** (295 King Street) exhibits Aboriginal art and artefacts, including possum-skin cloaks, and a dedicated oral history project preserves for future generations the oldest living culture in the world.

Melbourne's love affair with books began in 1835 with founder **JOHN PASCOE FAWKNER**, who housed the town's first library in his hotel. His statue, at the corner of Market and Collins streets, remembers a tribune of the people—a man who issued the fledgling town's first newspaper written by hand while he waited for a printing press to arrive.

Melbourne's newspapers are central to the story of our literary heritage. Most of the writers collected in this book have worked for a Melbourne newspaper, and the flat of Collins Street between Elizabeth and Swanston streets is the city's newspaper heart. **NEWSPAPER HOUSE** (247–249 Collins Street), adorned by Napier Waller's 1933 mosaic 'I'll put a girdle around the earth', was one of media magnate Rupert Murdoch's early offices.

Across the road and through collinstwo3four (234 Collins Street) is **HOWEY PLACE**. The iron and glass roof overhead is all that remains of Cole's Book Arcade—once 'the biggest bookstore in the world' containing more than a million books, a Chinese tea salon, a hall of funny mirrors, a fernery and a monkey enclosure. The eccentric proprietor was EW Cole, publisher of the classic *Cole's Funny Picture Book*.

South along Swanston Street at the corner of Flinders Lane is the Nicholas Building, which houses writers' and artists' studios as well as Kris Hemensley's **COLLECTED WORKS BOOKSHOP** (L1/37 Swanston Street)—a must visit for poets and readers of Australian poetry.

This stretch of Flinders Lane is a hub for independent publishers, designers and media makers, many of who keep studios here. Just west of the corner of Swanston Street is Degraves Street. Look for the subway stairs near the end of the street that descend to **STICKY INSTITUTE** (Shop 10, Campbell Arcade), where you can encounter Melbourne's vibrant underground publishing scene.

Coming up out of the subway, you'll find yourself at **FLINDERS STREET STATION**, one of the city's most recognisable landmarks. The station features prominently in numerous renditions of the city and the phrase 'I'll meet you under the clocks' is so common it has become a part of Melbourne's popular lexicon.

Across the road, head for Federation Square then east along the north bank of the Yarra River to **SPEAKERS' CORNER**—little mounds nestled among the trees at the far end of Birrarung Marr. Speakers' Corner was particularly popular in the late-nineteenth and early-twentieth centuries for lectures and protests—not least because Melbourne was without a city square until 1976.

Backtrack across the park toward the city and head north for Batman Avenue and Exhibition Street. Near the corner of Exhibition and Bourke streets is the **HILL OF CONTENT BOOKSHOP** (86 Bourke Street). Established by AH Spencer in 1922 it is Melbourne's oldest surviving bookstore, and has hosted eminent visiting authors and employed many local writers over the years.

Just east is Liverpool Street. Beguiling and mysterious, Melbourne's laneways feature prominently in our literature. Fergus Hume's 1886 novel *Mystery of a Hansom Cab* features detective Kilsip touring the bewilderingly dark and narrow lanes, muttering to himself that it is like walking in the shadow of the valley of death. Further north along Punch Lane is the forgotten precinct of **LITTLE LONSDALE**—where CJ Dennis's larrikins Ginger Mick, Digger Smith, the Bloke, Doreen and Rose dealt it out wiv bricks an' boots.

West along Little Lonsdale Street is the majestic **STATE LIBRARY OF VICTORIA** (328 Swanston Street)—the centre of Melbourne's literary activity since it opened in 1856. Access to the library has always been free: 'every person of respectable appearance is admitted, even though he be coatless … if only his hands are clean.' Peter Carey, Frank Hardy,

Ray Lawler and Arnold Zable have all written here, and the addition of the Centre for Books, Writing and Ideas in 2009 means many more will too. The opulent reading rooms are named for the driving forces behind the library: Charles Joseph La Trobe and Redmond Barry. Free tours of the library take in significant artefacts of Victoria's literary history.

North via Swanston Street is Carlton—the site of Helen Garner's 1977 novel *Monkey Grip* and home to the **UNIVERSITY OF MELBOURNE** as well as academics, writers and readers of all kinds. Vincent Buckley set his epic sequence *Golden Builders* here—in gaps of lanes, in tingling shabby squares—asking, 'Cardigan, Elgin, Lygon: shall I find here my Lord's grave?'

East at Queensberry Street is Carlton Gardens and the **MELBOURNE MUSEUM**, where you will find Fawkner's printing press as well as artefacts from Cole's Book Arcade. East via Gertrude Street is Atherton Gardens—the site of Tony Birch's *Shadowboxing*, which remembers Fitzroy street life before the towers.

East again is the suburb of **COLLINGWOOD**—the backdrop to Frank Hardy's *Power Without Glory*. This controversial novel, based on the life of Melbourne businessman John Wren, led to an unsuccessful prosecution for criminal libel in 1951. So vivid is Hardy's narrative that the book reads like a roadmap of inner Melbourne.

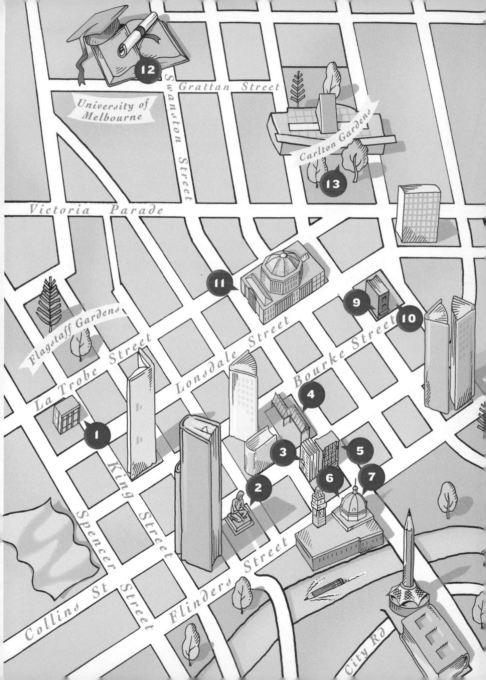

1. **KOORIE HERITAGE TRUST,** 295 King Street.

2. **JOHN PASCOE FAWKNER** statue, corner Market Street and Collins Street.

3. **NEWSPAPER HOUSE,** 247–249 Collins Street.

4. **HOWEY PLACE,** off Little Collins Street.

5. The Nicholas Building and **COLLECTED WORKS BOOK-SHOP,** 37 Swanston Street.

6. **STICKY INSTITUTE,** Shop 10, Campbell Arcade.

7. **FLINDERS STREET STATION,** corner of Flinders Street and Swanston Street.

8. **SPEAKERS' CORNER,** Birrarung Marr.

9. **HILL OF CONTENT BOOKSHOP,** 86 Bourke Street.

10. **LIVERPOOL STREET,** head north to Punch Lane and Little Lonsdale Street.

11. **STATE LIBRARY OF VICTORIA,** 328 Swanston Street.

12. **UNIVERSITY OF MELBOURNE,** corner of Swanston Street and Grattan Street, Carlton.

13. **MELBOURNE MUSEUM** and Carlton Gardens, 11 Nicholson Street, Carlton.

14. **COLLINGWOOD.**

LIST OF ILLUSTRATIONS

EXTRACT CREDITS

All text extracts have been reproduced with permission of the copyright holders or licensors. Specific acknowledgements have been requested regarding extracts from the following titles.

Academy Editions of Australian Literature editions of *The Recollections of Geoffry Hamlyn*, and *His Natural Life*, and *Robbery Under Arms* courtesy The Australian Academy of the Humanities and University of Queensland Press.

Colonical Texts edition of *The Pipers of Pipers Hill* and John Shaw Neilson *The Collected Verse* courtesy of Australian Scholarly Editions Centre, Australian Defence Force Academy.

The Fortunes of Richard Mahony by arrangement with the licensor, the Estate of Henry Handel Richardson, C/o Curtis Brown (Aust) Pty Ltd.

Cooper's Creek , copyright © Alan Moorehead 1963, 1977, 1985, reproduced by permission of Pollinger Limited and the estate of Alan Moorehead.

Tyranny of Distance, copyright © Geoffrey Blainey 1966, 1982, 2001, by permission of Pan Macmillan Australia Pty Ltd.

The Female Eunuch, © Germaine Greer 1970, 1971, by permission of HarperCollins Publishers Ltd.

Dancing With Strangers, © Inga Clendinnen 2003, and *Cafe Scheherezade* © Arnold Zable 2001, and *The Murray Whelan Trilogy*, © Shane Maloney, 1994, 1996, 1998, and *The Broken Shore*, © Peter Temple 2005 all by permission of Text Publishing.

Kickback © Garry Disher, 1991, The Ancestory Game © Alex Miller 1992 and Cocaine Blues © Kerry Greenwood 1989 by permission of Allen & Unwin.

Picnic at Hanging Rock and *Monkey Grip* reproduced with permission by Penguin Group (Australia).

True History of the Kelly Gang © Peter Carey, reproduced by permission of the author C/o Rogers, Coleridge & White Ltd., London.

The Art of the Engine Driver, © Steven Carroll reproduced by permission of HarperCollins Publishers.

Dead Europe by Christos Tsiolkas, 2005, Reprinted by permission of Random House Australia.

The Darkening Ecliptic by arrangement with the licensor, the Estate of James McAuley, C/o Curtis Brown (Aust) Pty Ltd. and with the Estate of Harold Stewart.

The Bee Hut © Dorothy Porter, Black Inc., 2009

Lenny Lower © Barry Dickins 1982, by permission of Barry Dickins. Denis Moore played the solo-part of Lennie Lower in Sydney and in Melbourne in 1982.

A Little Bush Maid by arrangement with the Licensor the Estate of Mary Grant Bruce C/o. Curtis Brown (Aust) Pty Ltd.

I Can Jump Puddles, and *Hating Alison Ashley*, and *The Gathering*, and *Animalia*, and *Sleeping Dogs* all reproduced with permission by Penguin Group (Australia).

Winter by John Marsden reprinted by permission of Pan Macmillan Australia Pty Ltd. Copyright © Jomden Pty Ltd 2000.

The Bad Book reprinted by permission of Pan Macmillan Australia Pty Ltd. Text copyright © Backyard Stories Pty Ltd 2004, Illustration copyright © Terry Denton 2004.

INDEX

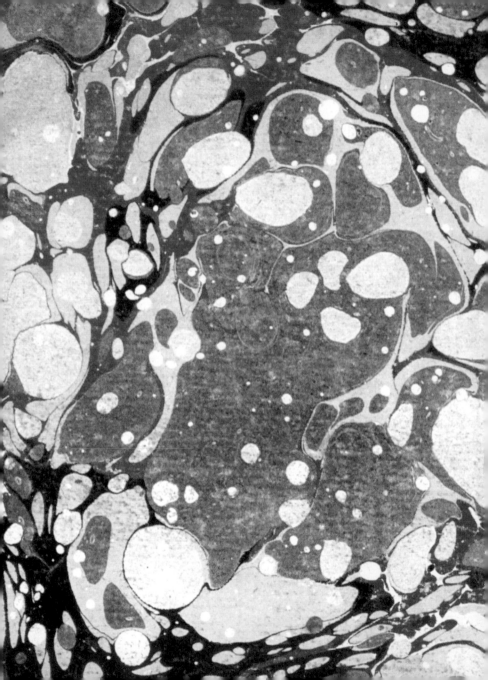